CIRCLES of HOPE

Breathing Life and Spirit into a Wounded World

Bill Cane

Illustrated by Ann Thiermann

ORBIS BOOKS

Maryknoll, New York 10545

The Catholic Foreign Mission Society of America (Maryknoll) recruits and trains people for overseas missionary service. Through Orbis Books, Maryknoll aims to foster the international dialogue that is essential to mission. The books published, however, reflect the opinions of their authors and are not meant to represent the official position of the society.

Copyright © 1992 by Bill Cane
For the illustrations, copyright © 1992 by Ann Thiermann
All rights reserved
Published by Orbis Books, Maryknoll, NY 10545-0308
Manufactured in the United States of America

Library of Congress Cataloging-in-Publication Data

Cane, Bill.
   Circles of hope : breathing life and spirit into a wounded world /
Bill Cane.
      p. cm.
   Includes bibliographical references.
   ISBN 0-88344-816-5
   1. Human ecology—Religious aspects—Meditations. 2. Church and
social problems—Meditations. 3. Conduct of life. 4. Simplicity—
Religious aspects. I. Title.
BL435.C36 1992.
261.8—dc20
                                      92-10629
                                          CIP

Contents

Acknowledgments

In writing a book on *Circles of Hope,* I had a long time to reflect on the circles of hope that kept me going while I was writing! Many of the people whose words and spirit were very present to me are now dead. Among them are Gregory Bateson, Hannah Arendt, Dorothy Day, Rollie Jones, Myles Horton and my own father. My wife Pat Mathes Cane and many friends not only contributed, but also sustained me while I wrote. Peggy Law, Peter and Betty Michelozzi, Judy Ress, David Molineaux, Amber Coverdale Sumrall, Will McClain, and Jim McGinnis responded to the manuscript even when it was in its most incoherent stages. Sarah Bhakti and Teddy Carney brought editorial order out of chaos. Ann Thiermann expressed in art what words cannot say. Friends from Latin America, some of whose lives were being threatened, kept me very aware of the life and death importance of the issues I was writing about. Page Smith and Richard Shaull, as well as Eugen Rosenstock-Huessy before them, placed me in an intellectual lineage of hope. Countless groups of people who are struggling to build a sane world, some of them in the most difficult circumstances, have kept my hope alive. To all of them, I am deeply grateful.

Foreword

If you know that something is terribly wrong with our world today but don't know what you can do about it; if you are fed up with old approaches to the problem and looking for alternatives; if you are tired of listening to old voices, and would like to hear a new one, I urge you to read *Circles of Hope: Breathing Life and Spirit into a Wounded World.*

In it, Bill Cane invites us to join others on a journey leading to deeper awareness of the circle of death in which our world is caught, and there experience a transformation that will allow us to participate in the creation of a new future. And he shows us how we can equip ourselves for this task: by calling upon resources available to us within ourselves, by developing a new relationship with nature, by living in community with others and in solidarity with the poor, and by drawing upon the rich spiritual heritage not only of Western Christianity but also of indigenous Americans and Eastern religions.

As I read this book, I realized that the author was encouraging me to move in a direction that I had already sensed was the right one. But in dialogue with him, I found that my horizons were being widened, and that I had new grounds for hope. My perspective on the present situation underwent a change, which led to a reorientation of my thought and action. Here I can mention only a few of the things that have contributed to this.

Cane helps us to see more clearly the forces that are producing so much suffering and death and that threaten to destroy life on this planet. And yet, as he does this, he declares that, as the situation becomes more difficult, we can have greater hope. He takes this stand because he believes that death can be followed by resurrection. He knows that, when the world is coming to an end, it is possible to believe in the world-to-come and to work with all our hearts to bring a new world into being. And in the midst of all the circles of death we know, he asks us to open our eyes to other circles, in which lifegiving actions create ripples that cover the earth and reach from one generation to another.

As old forms of political and social militancy falter, Cane urges us to seize this opportunity to build a new foundation for dynamic and radical action. He points the way toward a change of mind and heart and the cultivation of a new spirit. Thus the ongoing long-term struggle for social transformation will flow naturally out of a new experience of the fullness of life. As we undergo basic changes in our values, life style and relationships, and join hands with the poor and persecuted of the earth, we will find a new life in community, capable of nourishing and sustaining a difficult struggle. Integral to this grounding and transformation is a new sense of wholeness and connectedness with "the great circle of life" — with the earth and all people on it, including those of other generations, and with all that happens in any part of the world. "To think round and to think whole is the beginning of contemporary wisdom."

From this perspective, Cane leads us in an exploration of areas in which a struggle is going on between the forces of death and the forces of life. In each, he helps us see more clearly what is happening in patterns of events that are killing the spirit. But his primary focus is on the circle of life, in which new hope is emerging, and the pattern of a new world is beginning to appear.

The author spells out the crucial importance of the witness to truth amid the web of lies and deceit in which we are caught. He calls our attention to the power of the powerless as they join together and risk their lives in confronting the principalities and powers around them. He describes the small but promising efforts being made to create economic alternatives and redirect technological development from perfecting weapons of death to enriching life for all.

Cane's primary focus is on the circulation of the spirit throughout our world and from one generation to another, as unknown and unheralded individuals and small communities cultivate a new quality of life and relationship, and pass on this spirit as they touch the lives of others. In his exploration of this quality of existence, he focuses on the cultivation of our capacity to dream and live by visions of a new future. And he reminds us of the importance of circles of faith, in which we discover once again what it means to be the church: the "ecclesia" or the community of those "called out," who dare to abandon the familiar ways of ordinary existence in order to live toward the future and participate in creating something that does not yet exist.

Cane challenges us to take initiatives in creating small communities that can become such circles of life. Each chapter combines insights into what is happening and examples of new life emerging, with suggestions for group reflection, meditation, and action; it also indicates sources for going further in dealing with each topic. And throughout, he makes it clear that we are not engaged in academic study as an end in itself, but are embarked on a journey that must find expression in our daily life.

What most commends this book to me is the fact that, in it, the author is describing a way of life that he and his wife Pat incarnate. He speaks out of a long struggle to embark on an exodus from the structures and values of the established order, and to move slowly through incoherence to the shaping of an alternative lifestyle with the exciting new possibilities and the renewed energies it has brought. As the Canes moved away from their jobs in a metropolitan area to a piece of land in the country, on which they built a small house and explored possibilities of near subsistence living, they discovered that they could not only create new alternatives for themselves but also help others to do the same. From helping seniors plant their own gardens and helping Central American refugees find sanctuary, they extended their horizons to building networks of solidarity and service with Latin American women and with grassroots leaders of small popular movements in Latin America and the United States.

As unexpected opportunities continued to open up before them, their own lives were enriched and they became more hopeful. And as they discover how to "breathe life and spirit into a wounded world," they pass on a portion of that spirit to those of us who have the privilege of knowing them. In and through *Circles of Hope,* Bill communicates that spirit to a wider circle. And he does it in such a way that we are challenged not to copy what Bill and Pat have done but to pursue our own search for hopeful alternatives with the same determination and expectation.

RICHARD SHAULL

Introduction

We rejoice even in our difficulties, because we know that difficulties produce patience, and patience perseverance, and perseverance hope. And that hope does not let us down, because the love of God has been poured forth into our hearts by the Holy Spirit given to us.

—Romans 5:2-5

As I was writing this book, I received a letter from a leader of the indigenous movement in Ecuador. Thirty Indian leaders had been captured and tortured. "The situation is more difficult," he wrote, "but of greater hope." More difficult, but *of greater hope.* How could that be?

I was writing a book because the situation in our world has become so difficult to bear. The pain and the difficulty keep creeping up on us. Gregory Bateson, the anthropologist, cited the parable of the frogs. Frogs in a tub of water will jump out if the temperature of the water rises suddenly. But if the temperature of the water rises gradually, degree by degree, the frogs will not jump. They will stay in the tub until the heat kills them.

The tub has been heating up for some time. Day by day, the situation grows more desperate. But few people jump because the changes are not that perceptible. People don't see the missile systems, the hole in the sky, the poisons in the water. They don't see the 140 species that are disappearing each day. They don't see the tropical forests being demolished. Changes in weather patterns and global warming are incremental. People live with them.

The prophet Ezechiel was confronted with something much more tangible—a pile of dead bones—and was asked, "Can these bones live?"

A number of times, as I worked on this book, I found myself staring at a pile of dead bones—the 40,000 people who starve to death each day in a world of plenty; the victims of Bhopal and Chernobyl; the bodies of Salvadorans and Nicaraguans and Guatemalans, killed simply because they were community leaders or organizers of the poor; young Iraqi soldiers, buried alive as they writhed in the sand. I wanted to cry.

I mourned the death of nature. The Mediterranean, which twenty-five years ago yielded an abundance of fish, can now barely support life. The Adriatic is dying. The Blue Danube is a deadly grey.

I felt death lurking in our air and our water, in the massive hole in the sky and in the chemicals and poisons in the depths of the sea. A scientist who did original research on the destruction of the ozone layer said at the time, "My research is going fine. Unfortunately it means the world is ending."

That was often my feeling—a premonition of the end. In this dire situation, how can things be *of greater hope?*

Eugen Rosenstock-Huessy, the historian-philosopher, declared that we must believe in the end of the world because it is sure to come at least once during our lifetime and many times in the course of history! But we must also believe in *the world to come,* and work with all our hearts to bring that new world into being.

As I delved into the difficulty of a dying world, I began to trace patterns of a new world coming to life.

When Page Smith first began writing his eight-volume *People's History of the United States,* he felt that he might, like Edward Gibbon, be describing the rise and fall of an empire. What gave him hope was the long line of people who rose up again and again during our history to meet moral challenges. The future, he concluded, is full of danger — but it is also full of hope.

Crisis offers both danger and hope. The Sanctuary Movement had just received a major blow when I went to attend the first national Sanctuary conference in Tucson, Arizona. The Reagan administration, which was determined to send Salvadoran and Guatemalan refugees back to the terror from which they had fled, had infiltrated communities of faith and begun to arrest church workers who were protecting the refugees. In Tucson, we entered a large banquet room and joined a circle of one thousand people from all over the country. We were surrounding a huddled group of refugees, their faces covered with red bandanas. Television cameras were fixed on us. The energy was electric. In one sense, insurmountable power was directed against us. In another sense, that room was exploding with a power that no government official could contain. The situation had become more difficult, but *of greater hope.*

The present power-holders rely on armaments, technology, corporate money and public relations to bolster their power. But nuclear weapons, corporate takeovers and media management have not brought us to a greater hope. They have left us empty, on the verge of destroying ourselves.

We are a badly wounded planet in search of spirit — in search of the Wholeness that can restore us to life. God and the world have gone through a divorce, and we are the children of that divorce. The separation of spirit and matter has led us to ecological death and human horror. A world without spirit became a world of resources — a world in which people and raw materials can be used and discarded for power and profit.

Many people look to their political leaders to take care of things for them — to pass laws, to initiate programs. But legislation and massive clean-up efforts are very limited; they can slow down the disease, but they cannot cure it. A change of mind and heart has to take place *within us;* a spirit of life must replace a suicidal spirit. For we are losing more than bodies of water; we are losing our life-giving spirit.

We suffer from a body-mind disease. We cannot repair the hole in the ozone layer without filling the vacuum in our souls. Gregory Bateson put it well. The sickness of Lake Erie, he claimed, was not *in* the lake. It was not *inside* a physical body of water. Rather, it permeated the people and the businesses around the lake. The households and corporations surrounding the lake were infected with greed and carelessness, were part of a throw-away culture that had lost all sense of its sacred connection with nature. So cleaning up a lake does not solve the problem. The pollution is mental as well as physical. The spirit and actions of a circle of people have to change.

This book focuses on the life and spirit that is being born within our present situation. It does not envision calling a spirit down from the heavens, but rather drawing upon the spirit deep in the earth, the air, the trees and the water. Restoring our spirit involves electrifying our hearts and imaginations—plugging into the energy of the earth, forming circuits of people with spirit; creating sparks by bringing together thought and compassion, body and soul, science and dreams, God and the earth.

There was a time when a somewhat coherent moral and religious sense held our society together. That time is gone. We cannot simply hearken back to it, nor can we afford to live without a sense of the sacred. Our task is to animate the world with a new spiritual and moral sense, and to put that sense into personal and global action.

Such a task involves us all. This book is part of the process. Each chapter traces a pattern of events that threatens to kill the spirit, and then probes ways in which new life and hope can emerge. The information presented here is not all new, but the patterns into which it is arranged are. More information is not our greatest need right now; we need to digest the information available so that it does not overwhelm and paralyze us. We need to be able to place it side by side with a vision of a new world coming into being. Only then can we act effectively. We cannot do everything. But our particular contribution needs to nourish us as well as nourish the circles of life around us. Only then can we persevere in our action.

We all have contributions to make. That is why the book is interactive. Each chapter begins with a synthesis of what has been happening, followed by a reflection, a meditation, and suggestions for action. The process connects us with others who are living hopefully; and it places us in the context of a Whole that nourishes us, even as it calls us to find our own way of circulating life and hope.

It is vital that we direct our energies in a hopeful direction and that we be nourished by our action. In taking steps together to heal the earth, we find ourselves being healed. In attempting to serve the Whole, we find ourselves becoming whole again. In joining hands with the poor and the persecuted of the earth, we find a richness of spirit that we can never know by splendid isolation.

The ancient Hebrew word for spirit was *ruah,* which meant breath or wind. We can't see the wind, but we can feel it. When people die, we know something is missing: the breath of life is gone; they have lost their *ruah.* (We still say "God bless you" when people sneeze and momentarily "lose" their *ruah.*) We can't see spirit, but we can smell death in institutions just as we can sense the spark of life in someone's eyes; we can pick up creativity and life in a classroom or home or business just as we can feel the thud of a deadening dullness.

The spirit is creative and life-giving. In the beginning, the *ruah* of God hovered above the primeval waters. "God breathed into the everyman and the everywoman the *ruah* of life." The spirit eventually got separated from the breath of life on earth and placed in an invisible world above and beyond us. Now the power of the spirit in the earth and in all of us needs to be unleashed and channeled. That is the greater hope being called forth by the difficulty all around us.

The Wholeness that the Earth craves and millions of its people yearn for is as yet a dream. We see through a glass darkly, we cannot find the right words, we stumble. But we do have images and intuitions of Wholeness, and our hearts and souls cry out for integration and healing. Even though we have to grope our way along, we must be people of the dream, because the alternatives we see all around us are nightmares.

To begin moving, to join hands with other people of the dream, to share our hopes—this is what matters now. The dream will not remain a dream. Slowly, as we join hands, we will take steps together—the steps in faith that are needed to help the dream of the Earth become history.

The crisis of the earth cannot be solved with the same mentality that has given rise to the crisis. A new mentality is needed—a change of heart, a different spirit. And a new faith, a new hope and a new love.

That is why people who jump and form circles through which a living spirit can flow are so important right now. For the circulation of spirit in nature and history and politics and technology—and in all of us—is now our greatest hope.

1

It's a Round World

The power of the world always works in circles, and everything tends to be round.
— Black Elk

Whatsoever we sow, the same also shall we reap.
— St. Paul

What goes around comes around.

We are part of a great circle of life on earth. We are not separate little beings; we are connected.

I remember a black man, many years ago, trying to impress the circularity and connectedness of life upon a bishop. "The world is round," the black man kept repeating. "It isn't flat. You can't sweep your garbage over the edge of the world, because there isn't any edge. You can't push people over the edge when you don't want them around any more either. The world is round. And if you keep trying to shove stuff over the edge and push people over, you better watch out. Because the world is round, and sooner or later, they're all gonna come back up around the other side and bat your ass!"

To think round and to think whole is the beginning of contemporary wisdom. Billiard balls and controlled labora-

7

tory experiments may be predictable, but life is not. The May 1992 riots in Los Angeles were part of a decade of polarization and impoverishment that finally circled around and came back to us. We can no longer confine ourselves to thinking straight and separate. We have to begin to think round and whole. We will be forever dizzy, confused — and *dangerous* — until we begin to live round and live whole.

The great circle of life has many smaller circles within it. I am seated at the edge of a small circle of life right now, in our home that overlooks a little lake. I began to think of Lake Freedom as a circle of life about ten years ago, when the county devised a plan to drain the lake in order to take pictures of the dry lake bed. We gathered with neighbors to talk about the plan. Don Chandler, a farmer who has lived here for sixty years, said that if the lake were drained and the rains didn't come quickly enough to fill it, the willows would start growing in the lake bed and we'd never get rid of them. The fish, of course, would die. The egrets and terns and herons would stop coming because there would be no fish. The rodent population would increase if the birds of prey left. Without fish in the lake, pools of water would bring mosquitoes. A nearby farmer who irrigated with lake water would suffer. As we talked, it became apparent to me how all of us around this lake — two-legged, four-legged, winged and finned creatures — make up a circle of life. Tinker with one part of the circle, and every other part is affected.

The ecology most certainly circles round and round. When I was young, our family used to go to Yosemite National Park for vacation. At that time, Yosemite valley was relatively bug-free, because it was being sprayed with a new chemical that had wiped out malaria in Burma during World War II. It seemed to be a clear-cut instance of linear cause-and-effect: spray DDT and the mosquitoes die; without mosquitoes, no malaria. But the DDT kept going round and round. It found its way into water supplies and birds' eggs and mother's milk and led to a terrifying disruption of the circle of life.

Today, long after DDT and other clearly harmful pesticides have been outlawed for use in the United States, DDT is showing up in large quantities in mother's milk in Guatemala. Attempts to stop chemical companies here from shipping outlawed chemicals abroad have so far been unsuccessful. Outlawed poisons circle around and come back to us in coffee beans and bananas and produce from Latin America.

Radiation circles the earth. The fallout from nuclear test explosions in the atmosphere is still circling around and coming down on us in wind and rain. Andrei Sakharov, creator of the Russian hydrogen bomb and winner of the Nobel Peace Prize, estimated that for every megaton of nuclear explosion in the atmosphere, 10,000 people would die prematurely of cancer. If he was correct, over 6 million people have died prematurely so far. (James Lerager, "Soviet Victims of Nuclear Testing," *Earth Island Journal*, Fall 1990; a study commissioned by International Physicians for the Prevention of Nuclear War estimates that fallout from bomb testing will cause 2.4 million cancer deaths worldwide. Cf. *Radioactive Heaven and Earth: The Health and Environmental Effects of Nuclear Weapons Testing In, On, and Above the Earth*, Apex Press, NY, 1991.)

Nuclear waste from weapons production and from power plants keeps accumulating, and forty years of scientific efforts have found no safe way to store it. Lake Karachay has been so polluted by Soviet nuclear weapons dumping in the past, that someone who stands by its shores for an hour will die of radiation sickness within weeks. Irradiated uranium fuel from power plants is expected to reach 200,000 metric tons worldwide by the year 2000. Such fuel spends itself very slowly. It will still be radioactive — and dangerous — 10,000 years from now.

Automobile exhaust, radiation, and nuclear waste can't be shoved off the edge of the earth. They don't dissipate. They accumulate and circle around and eventually threaten life everywhere. The garbage our industrial world keeps trying to shove over the edge does come back and "bat our ass" — in the form of acid rain, polluted water, cancer and a hole in the ozone layer.

In history, events can take a long time to circle around and come back to us. In 1913, Great Britain, wanting to assure itself a steady supply of oil, installed the royal emirate to govern Kuwait. In 1954, to protect British and American oil interests, the CIA helped overthrow the democratically elected Mussadegh government of Iran and installed the Shah. The overthrow of the Shah, the rise of Islamic fundamentalism, the hostage crises, the militarism of Saddam Hussein, and war and crisis in the Persian Gulf were not simply "caused" by madmen over there. Our interference of decades ago also keeps circling around and coming back to us.

In a round world, even the dead come back to haunt us. When Stalin ordered mass executions, he often killed the firing squads so that no one would be left to tell the story. You would think that such murders would have been conclusive. But now, sixty years later, Stalin's victims are being dug up. The suppressed stories are being told in the former Soviet republics at this late date.

In Latin America over the past four decades, the military and secret police have been silencing popular protest by "disappearing" popular leaders. According to FEDEFAM, The Families of the Disappeared of Latin America, there are now about 100,000 *documented* cases of people being "disappeared" in Latin America. Disappearance is the ultimate way of trying to sweep people over the edge of the earth. It leaves no dead bodies, no evidence of murder, no record. The government and army and security police claim they know nothing. But even disappearances come back to haunt the governments who sponsor them. Zenaida Velasquez, whose brother was disappeared by the Honduran government in 1981, describes one of the repercussions — the protest marches. Twenty thousand women are marching in the streets

minded meditate about; compassion lies at the heart of life on this planet. What we do to others and to the environment, we sooner or later do to ourselves. For the self is not bounded by the skin, but is connected to a much larger SELF. It is not just altruism and love, it is also SELF-interest that will save us.

"Man did not weave the web of life," wrote Ted Perry in the spirit of Chief Seattle. "He is only a strand in it. Whatever he does to the web, he does to himself." The part can no longer make believe that it does not belong to the Whole or contribute to the life or death of the Whole. We are one great respiration, one great circulation, one great web of life over this round earth.

What Can We Do?

❧ REFLECTION ❧

Joseph Campbell, the great student of myth and symbol, felt that the most hopeful image we have to guide us right now is that of the Whole Earth, in which we see ourselves as part of a great Living Sphere.

- Picture yourself as part of the Whole Earth. Breathe in and breathe out, and picture the breath of life circulating through the trees and over the oceans and all around you and in you. Extend your arms in a circle, to embrace those near and dear to you. Reach up toward the clouds, open your arms to the sun, reach out to touch the trees that are purifying the air. Let the earth and the sky embrace and hold you as part of the great circulation of life on earth.

- Focus on daily routines that can contribute to the circulation of life or the clogging of the arteries of the earth—the garbage you produce, the water and energy you use, what you buy and consume—and connect the simple actions of recycling and of not buying frivolously with the health of the Whole.

⋙ LEARNING ⋘

Our diet circles the earth, as John Robbins points out in *Diet for a New America*. To cite just a few examples:

- Number of people who will starve each year: about 60,000,000
- Number of people who could be adequately fed by the grain saved if Americans reduced their meat intake by 10 percent: about 60,000,000

- Pounds of potatoes that can be grown on one acre of land: 20,000
- Pounds of beef that can be produced on one acre of land: 165

- Amount of meat imported annually by the United States from Costa Rica, El Salvador, Guatemala, Nicaragua, Honduras and Panama: 200,000,000 pounds
- Amount of meat eaten by average person in Costa Rica, El Salvador, Guatemala, Nicaragua, Honduras and Panama: less than the average American housecat

- A major contributor to the destruction of rainforests in Latin America: clearing for cattle ranches
- Thought to be a major contributing factor to cancer in the United States: high consumption of meat in the diet

⋙ ACTION ⋘

Cut down on meat in your diet. Eat lower on the food chain. Cook creatively with simple ingredients.

Support the "Circle of Poison" legislation. Let your elected representatives know that you do not want chemicals that are outlawed here to be exported to other countries.

⊰ SELF-INTEREST ⊱

Gregory Bateson felt that our society is addicted to the very things that are killing us. He compared us to the little creatures in *Alice in Wonderland* with the sugar-cube heads. When asked how they sustained themselves, they replied, "By dipping our heads in weak tea." "But doesn't that dissolve your heads?" asked Alice. The way we have been sustaining ourselves is eating away at our heads. It is in our own vital interest to change!

⊰ MEDITATION ⊱

In 1971, Ted Perry wrote a "Letter to the President in Washington" in the spirit of Chief Seattle, the eloquent Indian leader of the mid-nineteenth century. He drew upon the sayings of the Indian chief, but added his own ecological emphasis. An excerpt follows:

This land is sacred to us. We take our pleasure in the woods and the dancing streams. The water that moves in the brooks is not water but the blood of our ancestors. If we sell you the land, you must remember that it is sacred to us, and forever teach your children that it is sacred . . .

The rivers are our brothers; they quench our thirst. The rivers, between the tender arms of their banks, carry our canoes where they will. If we sell our land, you must remember, and teach your children that the rivers are our brothers, and yours, and you must henceforth give the rivers the kindness you would give to any brother.

What is it that the white man wishes to buy, my people ask me? The idea is strange to us. How can you buy or sell the sky, the warmth of the land, the swiftness of the antelope? How can we sell these things to you and how can you buy them? Is the earth yours to do with as you will, merely because the red man signs a piece of paper and gives it to the white man? If we do not own the freshness of the air and the sparkle of the water, how can you buy them from us? Can you buy back the buffalo, once the last one has died?

Teach your children what we have taught our children, that the earth is our mother. Whatever befalls the earth, befalls the sons of the earth. If men spit upon the ground, they spit upon themselves. This we know. All things are connected like the blood which unites our family. If we kill the snakes, the field mice will multiply and destroy our corn. All things are connected. Whatever befalls the earth, befalls the sons of the earth. Man did not weave the web of life; he is merely a strand in it. Whatever he does to the web, he does to himself.

⊰⊱ CELEBRATION ⊰⊱

In light of the destruction of life that is going on all around us, it is vital to celebrate the life that is still present, and the people all over the world who are protecting and furthering life.

- Make use of times like sunrise and sunset, a grace or toast before meals, a picnic or an outing to stop and appreciate the circulation of life all around us.

- Camping, walking in the woods, digging in a garden or planter box, dancing — all can be celebrations of the life that flows through all creation.

- Introduce ways to celebrate the connectedness of life in your church or community of faith. From their earliest years introduce children to a sense of the Whole, and their part in sustaining the life of the Whole.

⊰ FOR GROUPS ⊱

As a group, do a large drawing of the earth as seen from space and depict some of the destructive influences that are circling the globe (e.g., radioactivity, chemicals that are destroying the ozone layer, harmful pesticides, smog and pollution, acid rain, nuclear missiles, the proliferation of weapons, human rights abuses, economic exploitation, destruction of species, loss of forests).

Then do another drawing showing some healing influences that are circling the globe (e.g., peace groups, recycling efforts, solidarity groups, citizen diplomacy, intercultural exchange programs, disarmament, new technologies that do not pollute, efforts of the United Nations).

Lastly, do a drawing showing how both the destructive forces and the healing forces can flow through our daily lives (e.g., in the form of the energy we use, the garbage and smog we produce, the taxes we pay, the things we buy, the groups we belong to, how we treat each other, how we influence our elected representatives, our attitudes toward foreigners, our communities of faith and action).

Join hands as a group and visualize the power for wounding and healing the earth that flows through all of us.

⊰ RESOURCES ⊱

Lester Brown et al., *State of the World 1992: A Worldwatch Institute Report*, W. W. Norton and Co., New York, 1992.

Ted Perry, *Letter to the President in Washington*, Middlebury Magazine, Winter 1989.

John Robbins, *Diet for a New America*, Earthsave Foundation, 315 Quail Terrace, Ben Lomond, CA 95005.

The film *Brother Sun, Sister Moon* is available at many video stores.

Within the Womb of Gaia

2

In the Womb of Gaia

The Circle of Nature

That which goes against the way of the Tao will not survive.

— Lao Tzu

Nature is a nourishing and wise circle. Like babes in the womb, we are being nourished within that circle this very moment, as we breathe in the oxygen the circle provides for us. Outside of this circle, we cannot survive. We live, not as detached individuals, but as womb-mates—cooperative parts of the Whole.

Just down the road from us there are a number of large greenhouses with sensors sticking out from them. The sensors measure the temperature, the humidity and the light outside the glass houses and give this information to the computer inside. The computer already knows the time of day and the season of year, at what hour the sun is going down and when darkness will fall. With all this information, the computer keeps adjusting the temperature and light inside the greenhouses with one overall purpose—the well-being of the flowers.

Whenever we drive by and see the sensors sticking out of the greenhouses, we marvel at the balancing act going on inside. But it's nothing compared to the balancing act that is going on where *we* live. All around us there are gigantic sensors, involved in an intricate balancing act. The earth is always busy adjusting its temperature and humidity and oxygen level, so that we can stay alive. The sun and the earth keep their proper distances, so that we won't burn up or freeze to death. The trees and the oceans and the clouds and the winds and the rain keep circulating our water so that we won't dehydrate. Trillions of bacteria and earthworms work the soil so that it can produce lush vegetation. And like the computer's sensors, the clouds and the trees and the sun and the oceans communicate with each other to keep a relative balance that allows the flowers of life to blossom all over the earth.

The trees breathe in carbon dioxide and exhale oxygen. If there is an excess of CO_2 the oceans can absorb a lot of it, and ocean currents can take it down to the bottom of the sea. The clouds and the wind and the trees and the lakes and the oceans cooperate to keep our water recirculating. True, nature can be a destructive force — and there are floods and hurricanes and earthquakes — but all in all, nature provides a balance that sustains and furthers life.

The system has worked for aeons. But now, it is as if delinquents have broken into the greenhouses and begun sabotaging the computer. The earth's balancing act is being thrown off. It can't keep the air or the water clean or the ozone layer intact. It can't circulate the water adequately because there is so much forest missing. We have been engaged in very subtle acts of terrorism — not against the government, but against life on earth.

I must confess that I grew up with little appreciation for the marvellous balancing act that sustains us. My limited introduction to nature was in our tiny backyard in San Francisco where we chewed lemon grass and popped fuschias and went "Ughh" when we saw a bug. For us, the snails and bees and spiders and worms were simply pests to be eliminated by sprays and poisons. Weeds were enemies. Flowers were beautiful, but always in danger of wilting or being eaten by bugs. I didn't spend a lot of time in the backyard; I spent it on concrete and asphalt and lawn.

Some thirty years later, my wife Pat and I acquired a much larger backyard—six acres in Santa Cruz County, California. My ideas about nature had changed considerably by that time, but my experience hadn't. I remember our neighbor Tony perched on his backhoe, clearing a building pad for our house, asking me a question, "Should I take these trees out?" I stared up at the trees and realized I didn't even know what they were. My initial impulse was: "Yes, clear everything!" But caution prevailed. "Let's leave them for now." "They" turned out to be wild lilac and oak, beautiful trees which I now treasure. The lilacs bloom lavender in the spring, and the oaks house hundreds of tiny warblers and chickadees. My practical relationship with nature—a time of living round and living whole—had begun.

One of our mentors at that time was Quin Hill, an artist who ran the "Flora-Fauna" saw mill but who didn't like to cut down trees! The mill was not listed in the phone book and was hidden away on a remote road in the Santa Cruz Mountains, with a redwood sign that was virtually invisible. Quin was nestled in his little forest hideaway working on all sorts of projects that fascinated him, occasionally commenting that "the lumber business is lousy!"

We found Quin by an accident we always considered providential. When we were looking for someone to mill lumber from our trees, an old-timer at one of the commercial mills remembered his name. Quin had lived up in the mountains without electricity for fifteen years. Twenty-five years before that, he had been an artist and architect in the San Francisco Bay Area. He was able to thin our groves selectively, mill our lumber and draw the plans for our house.

Quin also helped us to identify the trees and wild plants on the land. Under his tutelage, I began to appreciate the variety and wisdom of nature. I began to realize that the trees are part of the sensitive and responsive circle of life. Trees are our external lungs — our lungs extract oxygen from the air; the trees put the oxygen back in. If you look carefully at their branches, you will see that trees are even shaped like lungs, except that their branches reach up, rather than hang down. The redwoods on our land have been here for hundreds of years, cleansing the air, and breathing out hundreds of gallons of water each day. They can cut back, in a drought year, to 10 percent of their usual growth rate. They can grow a new foot to balance themselves if the bank on one side of their root system slips away. The more I have lived among the redwoods, the more I have realized that I am surrounded by wise and venerable friends.

Most of our six acres we left wild. The foxes, the deer, the owls, the herons and other creatures inhabit it. When a group of students from the University of California at Santa Cruz did a study of the plant and animal life around the lake, Ken Burton identified over 120 species of birds that visit us each year. We rejoice in the elderberries that the band-tailed pigeons come to eat, the fruits, nuts, berries and seeds that grow wild and feed the earth's creatures.

As my childhood horror of spiders and bees and weeds slowly dissipated, I began to see them as part of the marvellous circuitry of nature, part of the swirl through which life flows. I now appreciate the bees pollinating the fruit trees as they gather nectar and pollen; the spiders, lady bugs and tree frogs eating garden pests; the trees spreading their foliage to the sun; the lake and the trees exhaling mists that return to form clouds that will water the earth. I see the ants carting away garbage, and I listen to the hoot of the owls and the squawk of the herons that prey on our numerous rodents. The cycles of nature are now an integral part of our lives, and we can feel the seasons circling around and renewing the earth.

We include ourselves as part of the cycle of life. We planted fruit trees, raspberries, asparagus and seasonal vegetables. When we pick things to eat now, we know that the earth is the real source of our nourishment, not the supermarket. We feed the chickens our kitchen garbage as well as weeds and cuttings from the land. They pick out their nourishment and at the same time add their body wastes to make a wonderful compost. Then we put the compost in the garden to nourish the vegetables. When we eat the vegetables, the cuttings and the waste and the weeds go right back to the chickens, and the cycle begins again.

I am slowly learning to live in communion with and nourish the great natural systems of which I am a part. I have begun to love the Whole. Augustine used to begin his prayer with the statement, "Someone wishes to praise you, Lord—someone who is a tiny speck of your creation." That's what we are—tiny specks. As parts of the Whole, we will never understand the Whole, but within the Whole we live and move and have our being.

When I meditate now, the redwoods, the birds, the lake, the sun, the moon and the clouds are very much a part of the meditation. We have become a community breathing in and out and giving thanks together. The sap of the redwoods, the scent of the orange blossoms, the hovering of the hummingbird have somehow gotten into my bloodstream. We nourish each other.

The urban scientific mindset I grew up with led me to believe that I was separate from the earth, that I could stand outside and study it, break it down into atoms and chemical constituents and control its processes. I could spray it with poisons if I wished and make as much garbage as I felt like. But now I know I am not on the earth, observing it; I am inside, being whirled around and receiving nourishment like one of many babes in a giant womb. I can feel the circulation of life and energy flowing through me and around me, just as I can feel my heart and my blood pressure and my breathing. I sense the earth re-circulating our air and our nutrients for us, and keeping our temperature livable. At times I can feel all of nature breathing in and out together. I realize that animals and plants are not "inanimate" or "dumb," but are part of a living Whole filled with wisdom and spirit.

This Whole, which the British scientist James Lovelock has called "Gaia" (after the Greek Goddess of the Earth), is not outside of us: we are all parts of Gaia or "Pacha Mama" as the Quechua Indians call our mother earth. For the Quechuas, the sun is father, the earth is mother and we are all relatives.

We exist only as part of a living, breathing Whole that is much wiser than we are — a Whole that can nourish and sustain and teach us. By pretending to be separate, I found that I had been cutting myself off from the wisdom and the life-pulse of the Whole. "The Spirit of God fills the entire earth," says an ancient Christian hymn. Cut off from the Whole, we human beings are fools bent on our own destruction. "That which goes against the way of the Tao (the Great Mother)," wrote Lao Tzu, "will not survive." St. Paul was writing about a community when he declared that we are all members of one body, dependent upon each other. But what he said of the community applies equally well to the living, breathing earth. "Can the hand say to the foot," asked Paul, "I have no need of you?" To amputate one part of the living sphere sends shivers throughout the rest of the sphere. We are all members of one living body.

The poets and mystics recognized our kinship with a sacred living Whole. Francis of Assisi spoke of brother sun and sister moon; he addressed earth, air, fire, water and animals as his relatives. He spoke to creation in song and poetry and prayer.

I have finally begun to have conversations with Gaia — to open my heart and get in touch with the life and breath of Gaia that flows through all of us. I share her joy and exuberance and feel her pain. I wince now, as I realize that 140 species are condemned to death each day. I can feel the bite of the chain saws chewing down the tropical forests at the rate of fifty to one hundred acres per minute. When I look up into the sky and imagine a hole in the ozone layer that is now twice the size of the continental United States, I feel desperate.

I sense a kinship with those who are trying to keep the circulation of life flowing—the friends and protectors of Gaia. With Chico Mendez in Brazil who organized the rubber tappers and tried to save part of the Amazon from big agricultural developers. Mendez was a peasant who never went to a formal school, but he knew that the devastation of the Amazon would affect weather patterns all the way to France. In 1988 he was gunned down by ranchers who wanted to fell the trees and grow beef for export.

In 1990, representatives of eight groups of Bolivian Indians marched out of the jungle through the sweltering heat of the tropics and into the cold of the altiplano. Government representatives tried to persuade them to go back to their forests. But eight hundred strong, they kept marching for over a month until they reached the capital city of La Paz. Thousands of people were lining the streets of the city shouting "Long live the courageous ones!" as the Indians solemnly marched through the city. The Indians demanded that the government put a stop to the logging of their ancestral lands. The Catholic church and the labor unions supported them, and the government had to back down and stop the big logging companies from devastating their tropical forests.

In 1991, I had the privilege of spending three weeks with a leader of the indigenous Indian movement in Ecuador. For the Quechua Indians, the earth is truly Pacha Mama, our mother. "How can you sell your mother?" they ask. "How can you cut her up and sell her?" The Quechuas feel that they must apologize to a tree if they have to cut it down.

The roots of American Indian spirituality go back thousands of years. The spirit of the indigenous peoples has been passed on from generation to generation and has survived five hundred years of European conquest. Their dream is control over their land and their forests and their ecology. They see tribes sharing land in common, so that all will be able to survive, and individuals will not fight one another over land. It is easy to dismiss such utopian notions as dreams that have long since vanished, until we realize that the Indians make up 44 percent of Ecuador's population. During the 1980s the tribes united. In 1990 they practically shut down the country with their demonstrations because the government would not dialogue with them. In Peru and Bolivia and other countries, the Indians are also rising up, making demands that are both political and ecological. They are attempting to live out the values passed on to them by their ancestors.

I have visited little watershed groups in the forests of northern California who do ecological research and challenge the permit applications of the big logging companies. They band together when Georgia Pacific or Louisiana Pacific move in to take down the old growth forests. The little circles of people out among the trees grew from one group in 1988 to over twenty groups in 1991. They were a crucial part of the movement that led to increased pressure for new timber legislation in California. Such groups seem small and insignificant, but the spirit that breathes in these movements is powerful and worldwide.

I have a new sense of religion. "Loving the Lord God with all your strength and all your soul" is a fairly abstract notion. But embracing the earth and all the creatures on it—the circle of life that includes the trees and birds and dolphins and peoples—is at once a very earthy and a very spiritual passion. It makes Democratic and Republican platforms, political and corporate agendas, pale. It means being part of a sacred circle and continually finding ways to protect and nourish that circle.

The contribution that any one of us can make may seem very small. But the first steps are placing ourselves in the embrace of the Whole, giving thanks and letting ourselves be nourished. We can increasingly become part of the circuitry through which life flows, rather than the obstructions that are clogging it up. By recycling our garbage, avoiding throw-away plastics, living more frugally, we allow our little circles of life to breathe more easily. By joining hands across racial and religious and national boundaries, we can imbibe the spirit of peoples who had a keen sense of Pacha Mama long before Columbus came to the Americas. The spirit with which we all act eventually circles the earth and strengthens the bond that is growing among us.

We are a destructive as well as a creative race. Call it original sin, call it illusion or addiction, call it the human condition — we always have to deal with a tragic story. But there is a thread of goodness, hope and renewal within that tragic story. The spirit of solidarity with the Whole is growing all over the earth. There are martyrs. And there are many people whose names and stories we do not know who are working and pleading and caring. The Whole of which we are parts has her own wisdom and embraces us all. We can draw energy from each other and from our communion with the Whole as we attempt to stop the devastation and the greed that surround us.

As a race, we are the consciousness (and conscience) of Gaia. We *are* the Earth becoming more and more conscious of herself. We can not only feel her pain and her beauty; we can share it and put it into words and action. Human beings may be devastating the earth, but human beings remain the earth's hope. With hands joined together locally and globally we are now one of the earth's crucial life-support systems. "We will begin," wrote Teilhard de Chardin, "to live constantly in the presence of and with the thought of the whole. There is nothing more significant ... than the spontaneous appearance, and ultimately, the systematic cultivation of a 'cosmic sense' of this kind."

What Can We Do?

✤ REFLECTION ✤

I sometimes draw imaginary circular lines that connect the fruit I am eating to the trees and the pollen and the bees and the rain and the sun and the soil — making the circulation of life's nutrients through us and through the living beings around us more obvious.

- Before meditating, I place myself within the womb of Gaia. I talk to the Whole and at times I become lost in the Whole.

- Breathe in and breathe out, aware that you are breathing the air that Gaia provides for us. The energy you feel, your sexuality, your ability to heal — all are part of a larger life that flows through us and around us. Let yourself feel part of this larger flow. Begin to talk *with* Gaia. Thank her and appreciate her. Feel her spirit throbbing within you.

- Spend time with a flower, among the trees, at the park. The womb of Gaia can nourish us, heal us and give us new life, if we let her.

✤ LEARNING ✤

- In our major U.S. cities, one out of four babies comes from the womb drug-addicted. (Outside of the cities, the ratio is one in ten.) Those who live in the giant womb that nurtures life on earth are also addicted — to fossil fuel, chemical wastes and poisons.

• Our addiction to poison and nuclear and fossil fuels is not necessary. Clean and renewable energy sources are available. The total amount of sun, wind, water and geothermal sources accessible to us in the United States is more than two hundred times our energy use and more than ten times our recoverable reserves of fossil and nuclear fuels, according to the U.S. Department of Energy.

• The Union of Concerned Scientists estimates that clean and renewable sources — sun, wind and water — could supply 50 percent of U.S. energy needs by the year 2020.

• Yet the Bush administration energy policy provides no significant funding for development and research into renewable energy sources! The entire emphasis is on fossil fuels and nuclear power — on dangerous and lethal addictions!

⋙ ACTION ⋘

• Cut down on consumption. Live simply so that others may simply live.

• Teach children from their earliest years to love and reverence the earth, to be frugal. Get the message into communities of faith and schools and community organizations.

• Eat less meat, recycle, use waxed paper or covered containers instead of plastic wrap, take cloth shopping bags to the supermarket.

- Dig in the garden or in a planter box or window box. Build up a little bit of soil. Nourish Gaia and let Gaia nourish you. Avoid pesticides and poisons. There are many natural remedies around these days. Consider buying organic vegetables and fruit if you cannot grow them yourself. If you have a yard, put your wet kitchen garbage, leaves and weeds into a compost pile.

- Put pressure on your elected representatives to stop sending armaments around the world and instead put the money into renewable energy sources and into making life livable for all the peoples of the earth. Write to your Congressional representatives. You don't have to be an expert to tell them how you feel.

❖{ SELF-INTEREST }❖

"If I am not for myself, who will be? But if I am only for myself, what am I?"
— Rabbi Hillel

- Our skin (Gaia's protective covering) is being torn away. A scientific panel convened by the United Nations Environment Program expects the frayed ozone layer to cause 1.6 million new cases of cataracts a year by the turn of the century (*San Jose Mercury News,* November 16, 1991). When you are exposed to the sun for long periods of time, wear sunglasses with sides that filter out UV-B and UV-A rays. Use sunblock (#15 or better).

- Our digestion (Gaia's digestion) is in trouble. Separate your garbage. Avoid buying throwaway items. Precycle! Try to cut garbage off at the source by avoiding plastic and styrofoam packaging.

- Our lungs (Gaia's lungs) are overburdened. You can help by buying appliances that conserve energy, driving less, getting better mileage, walking, taking public transport when you can. Use water, paper and electricity frugally. Buy only rechargeable batteries. Consider installing solar panels to heat household water. Replace regular light bulbs with the new fluorescent bulbs that cut electrical use by 75 percent and save you money in the long run. They are available from *Real Goods* (see Resources).

⊰{ MEDITATION }⊱

Thich Nhat Hanh, the Buddhist monk whom Martin Luther King nominated for the Nobel Peace Prize, provides us with individual ways to meditate in *Walking Meditation* (Fellowship Publications, New York, 1985) and *The Miracle of Mindfulness* (Beacon Press, Boston, 1975).

He invites us to walk as we meditate and make every step a conscious step upon the sacred earth, the mother of us all. Every step can be a step in reverence and peace, if we are striving for peace in our own lives.

He has devised a "stoplight meditation." When you have to stop for a traffic light, he suggests that instead of cursing the red light, you use it as a reminder to stop your inner churning, breathe in and breathe out, and say "Present moment, wonderful moment!"

When the phone rings, he advises us to take a moment to breathe in, breathe out, and appreciate our connection to all of life.

He tells us that something as simple as peeling and eating an orange can be a celebration of life, if only we are aware of the color, the skin, the juice, the taste. If we live in anxiety or hatred or jealousy, we cannot celebrate or appreciate the wonder of the orange!

⊰{ CELEBRATION }⊱

Pablo Casals always played a favorite piece of music when he awoke as a blessing on the day. Each morning, greet the new day with a blessing and a thanksgiving. Do the Yoga "Salute to the Sun," or some Tai Chi movement, or a simple stretching out of your arms to the sun and the sky.

Earth Prayers, edited by Elizabeth Roberts and Elias Amidon, is a collection of 365 poems, prayers and reflections that can be used every day before dinner, or as a meditation or blessing on the day (Harper Collins, San Francisco, 1991).

⇥ FOR GROUPS ⇤

Have each member of the group choose a different part to play in the life-giving action of nature (e.g., wind, rain, sun, clouds, trees, bees, birds, fish, animals, and human beings). Have the different players identify themselves by wearing signs or symbols of their part in nature. Prepare and perform a dance or pantomime that shows the constant cooperation and collaboration of the different parts of nature to sustain life on earth.

⇥ RESOURCES ⇤

Pierre Teilhard de Chardin, *Building the Earth,* Dimension Books, Wilkes-Barre, PA, 1965.

The *Earth Island Journal* is a quarterly that keeps you in touch with environmental news worldwide and with the latest developments in alternative technology. *Earth Island Journal,* 300 Broadway, Suite 28, San Francisco, CA 94133.

Real Goods publishes an alternative energy catalogue, which keeps you up to date on what is actually available at this point in time. Energy-saving fluorescent light bulbs can be ordered from this catalogue. *Real Goods,* 966 Mazzoni Street, Ukiah, CA 95428, 1-800-762-7325. (If you live in northern California, Pacific Gas and Electric Company sells the new fluorescent light bulbs at a great discount to its customers through its Save Energy Company, 2410 Harrison St., San Francisco, CA 94110, 415-824-6010.)

The *Worldwatch* Papers are an invaluable source of information on how our world is doing. Each pamphlet is about fifty pages long; topics range from renewable energy to water use, from the housing crisis to population growth. Worldwatch also publishes a magazine and an annual "State of the World" report. Worldwatch Institute, 1776 Massachusetts Avenue NW, Washington, D.C. 20036.

Passing on the Spirit

3

At the Heart of History

The Circulation of Spirit

Even in the darkest of times we have the right to expect some illumination, and such illumination may well come less from theories and concepts than from the uncertain flickering and often weak light that some men and women, in their lives and in their works, will kindle over the time span given them on earth.

— Hannah Arendt

The Chinese envision "meridian" lines that carry energy throughout the human body. History has its own "meridian" lines through which life and spirit flow from one generation to the next, and from one part of the world to another. We are an essential part of that transmission of spirit from place to place and from generation to generation.

History is not merely a chronicle of events that go on outside of us. History can flow *through* us—from people who have touched our hearts to people whose hearts we touch.

We can all look back and point to an aunt or an uncle or a parent or a teacher or a friend who touched us and gave us life. The man who touched me the most during my college years was an Alsatian priest whom we called "Pop" Phillips. At the time, I considered Pop fascinating and admirable — but eccentric. I had no idea that he was passing a living spirit on to me.

During the Great Depression of the 1930s when Pop helped organize poor farmers and farmworkers, he was accused of being a communist. "When you threaten the powers that be," he told us, "the first thing they say is that you are crazy. Then when other people join you, you are not so crazy any more — you become a threat, and they go after you. But when you get as old as I am, they don't bother you any more. You can do anything you want, and they don't give a damn!"

A few young priests who worked with Pop Phillips in the 1940s later trained Cesar Chavez and other future leaders of the United Farmworkers' Union of the 1960s. By that time, Pop was dead, but his spirit was alive in their efforts. Another priest whom Pop influenced, Hugh Donahue, later became a bishop and played a crucial role in getting Catholic church support for the United Farmworkers in California.

When I first knew Pop in the early 1950s, he had retired as pastor of St. Mary's Church in Oakland and was running Sunshine Camp, a summer camp for poor children. As college and seminary students, we formed a circle devoted to providing vacations for inner-city kids. We dug septic tanks, repaired plumbing, built cabins and planned all the activities for the children. We took them on outings to the Russian River, Jenner beach and the roller-skating rink.

Whenever someone came to visit camp, we relished introducing the new student to Pop, whose typical welcome went something like this: "I am very glad to meet you. That fence over there needs repairing. There is a hammer in the shed and you will find nails on the bench." "Salvation through sweat" was the gospel he preached to us.

In the 1950s, he was involved in sending pregnant cows

and goats to poor countries. He rebelled against pesticides and chemical agriculture even then, because he felt the poor people would get hooked on the new chemicals and big agribusiness would eventually take over. He preached the necessity of natural means of farming, especially extolling the virtues of the nitrogen cycle, which he called the "shit cycle."

I remember driving him into town once when he suddenly asked me to pull into a lumber yard. Pop pointed to a well-weathered pile of two-by-sixes and asked, "Are you using that pile of lumber over there?" Before the confused man could explain that it was for sale, Pop broke in, "If you are not using it, you do not deserve to own it. I need it to build a cabin for poor children." He saw the goods of the earth as things to be circulated for the good of those who really needed them. He wanted his kids to enjoy sunshine, good food, love and care, because it was their only time out of the inner city. They didn't pay for camp; they paid only what they could afford. Pop raised the rest of the money. Nobody who worked there received a salary. Pop always figured it was a privilege to be able to work for the poor!

He was a bag of bones with a determined spirit. His business card read: "Still alive at 75 on borrowed blood and borrowed time!" As college students, we used to donate our blood for him since he had pernicious anemia and needed regular transfusions. He thanked us once in a sermon: "These young men are giving me their blood, and I am very grateful to them, but as Our Lord himself once said, 'You cannot put new wine into old goat skins!' "

We took Pop to the hospital just before he died. "Oop, it's the beginning of the end," he said, "but that's all right." As we wheeled him down the hospital corridor, he began giving mock blessings as if he were the pope being carried on a *sedia gestatoria*. When an officious nurse came in to take his temperature, Pop pulled the thermometer out of his mouth, stared into her eyes and said, "Smile, damn you, smile!" The last words he said to us were, "Thank you for taking care of me. And remember, you will never find a better life than one that serves God's poor."

At the funeral, a little boy with big eyes asked me, "Will there be a camp now that Father Phillips is dead?" I choked back the tears and said, "Yes." The camp ended five years later, but the opportunity to keep Pop's spirit alive has arisen again and again.

A few years after Sunshine Camp closed, I had a chance to help start a camp myself — a camp for deaf children. I used to look at that camp and see Pop there, see his spirit hovering around the place. He had an iron certainty that a life of service was right, and he passed that certainty on to us.

Entering the spirit of history means becoming part of the nourishment — part of the life-giving transmission of spirit over generations. We are all at our best when we touch each other's hearts and give each other life. What really matters in history is people sharing life with others — not just physical life, but wisdom and love and a sense of service.

Historian Page Smith has a favorite story that illustrates how a living spirit was passed on for over one hundred years of American history. The story begins with Abraham Lincoln. Jane Addams's father was a good friend of Lincoln, and the spirit of Lincoln and his abolition of slavery deeply influenced Addams's life. As a little girl, Jane came home from school one day in 1865 to find her father weeping. "The greatest man in the world has been killed," her father told her. His friend Lincoln had been assassinated.

Jane grew up and went to the best of schools, but after finishing college she felt lost and depressed. On a tour of Europe, in the slums of London, her heart was touched by miserable creatures fighting over rotten vegetables, and she decided to devote her life to helping poor immigrants in the slums of the United States. She founded Hull House in Chicago in 1889, and then a series of settlement houses for immigrants in major cities of the United States.

Thirty years later, in the 1920s, Myles Horton was thinking

of starting a center in Appalachia where the whites and the blacks of the South could come together. He went to consult Jane Addams, and was deeply influenced by what she was doing. In 1930, he established Highlander Folk School in Tennessee.

Another twenty-five years went by, and Horton phoned Martin Luther King, Sr., to ask if there might be a young black person in Atlanta who would benefit from a session at Highlander. King said yes, he did have a young woman in mind by the name of Rosa Parks. Rosa Parks went to Highlander, and two months later made the momentous decision that touched off the civil rights movement in the United States. She later claimed that her experiences at Highlander were crucial influences in her decision not to step to the back of the bus!

The passing on of this sort of spirit from one generation to another—from Lincoln to Jane Addams to Myles Horton to Rosa Parks, from the Emancipation Proclamation of 1863 to the civil rights movement of the 1960s—is what history is all about. And it is what life is all about, too—inheriting a spirit and sharing it and passing it on to others.

My wife Pat and I met Myles Horton in Nicaragua in 1988. At that time, Myles was focusing his attention on Latin America and Africa, and he had dreams of building people-to-people bridges between rich and poor countries. "The multinationals have made it one world for business," he was saying, "so our job is to make it one world for people."

After Myles died, we helped carry on his vision by working with Phil McManus to bring a group of Latin American Christian base community leaders to meet some of their counterparts here in the United States. Guy and Candie Carawan, along with Lewis Sinclair, coordinated a trip through the deep South and a weekend at Highlander Center. Rodolfo Robles, a labor union leader from Guatemala, was so impressed with his experience at Highlander that he returned to found Casa CAMI, a miniature version of Highlander in

Guatemala City. Myles's spirit continued to move around the world.

Myles was aware that there are long periods in history when all we can do is nourish a tiny spark. And that spark may look hopeless in comparison to the cold and the dark all around us. But nourishing the spark, against all odds, keeps our spirit alive and gives our lives meaning. When the time comes, the igniting of many sparks gives history a meaning.

Sometimes the sparks come together and create an explosion, as they did in the 1960s in the United States and more recently in the Philippines, South Africa, Eastern Europe, the Soviet Union and China. Revolution is very close to hell, historian Rosenstock-Huessy tells us, but it is very close to heaven also, because it opens out a new future when the structures of society have been suffocating life and cutting off hope. We can see a new spirit struggling to be born in the former Soviet republics, in the pro-democracy movements in China and Eastern Europe, in the anti-apartheid movement in South Africa and in the movements of the poor in Latin America. These movements give all of us hope by opening new possibilities. The image of a lone Chinese student standing in front of a tank still burns in our memories. By protesting nuclear madness in the Soviet Union, Andrei Sakharov enlivened the peace movement here in the United States. Visits to Christian base communities in Latin America have set thousands of people here afire. The spirit is contagious.

The great eruptions, the ones that breathe a new spirit into large sectors of humanity, get put into the calendar and become a part of our yearly cycle of celebrations. The Passover celebrates the revolt of Moses and the Jewish people against the imperial power of Pharaoh. Christmas and Easter celebrate the victory of Jesus over the powers of domination, darkness and death. July Fourth celebrates our own revolution, and May Day in most parts of the world celebrates the Workers' Revolution. Things cannot happen everywhere all at once, but once they occur in one place, their influence can work its way around the globe. The American labor movement would not have been possible had not the Russian Revolution preceded it. The women's movement of the 1960s is now being felt all over the world. The inclusion of Martin Luther King, Jr., in our own calendar gives us hope that the spirit of freedom and justice is still alive in the United States.

The great rebirths in history are our spiritual heritage — they belong not just to Jews or Christians or Russians or Americans or brown or black people. The spirit of every revolution is incarnated in one place but belongs to us all. In our house, we have not only traditional icons but also modern ones of Gandhi, Martin Luther King, Jr., Dorothy Day, Archbishop Romero of El Salvador, and Mother Jones who led marches of children and women in the American labor movement.

I often talk to the spirits of the dead because they are much more alive than many of the people I see walking around me! They are present to me in my reflections and decisions, as are friends who are struggling for human rights in Peru, Honduras, Ecuador, Brazil, South Africa, Nicaragua and Guatemala. The struggle becomes less lonely, and some of the emptiness all around us gets filled by the presence of those who are far away, but whose spirit we share.

Page Smith tells us that his hope was restored by the constant emergence of people in our history who kept the spirit alive and passed it on. "When you know of the trials and tribulations of people in different periods of American history, and when you see history as a tragic drama, as I do — and against this backdrop, you still see the patience of some people, the faith and persistence with which they have continued to pursue some higher vision — when you see a long spread of this over decades and generations, then I think hope is inevitable!"

When we get a sense of the spirit pulsing through history, we can begin to look at our own lives, not just as separate and individual spans, but as part of this great circulation of life from country to country and generation to generation. Life takes on a greater urgency, a deeper meaning and a new zest. Talking to each other, raising children, writing letters and giving each other hugs become not isolated events but sparks that circulate around us. Inspiring and being inspired, remembering those who have gone before us and touching those who come after us—all become part of the circulation of life and spirit through space and time.

What Can We Do?

⁓{ REFLECTION }⁓

Take some paper and a pen and write down the names of two people—one well-known, another known perhaps only to yourself—who have passed a spirit on to you.

Choose one of these persons, and begin to say something to them in writing. Then write down what you hear them saying back to you, and then respond. Keep the dialogue going back and forth. Write whatever comes to mind. If you reach an impasse, simply write whatever you are feeling as part of the dialogue, for example, "I don't know what to say . . ."

When the conversation is finished, read it aloud to yourself and then write down your reactions to what you hear—your feelings as you listen to what has been said.

Lastly, thank the person for passing on a spirit to you. And plan to stay in touch with people you can encourage and nourish.

⁓{ LEARNING }⁓

- George Washington, in his Farewell Address, warned us that our future integrity as a country would depend upon our steering clear of the international intrigues and of the corruption that had been the downfall of the European powers. Two hundred years later, we find that our recent history is a chronicle of intrigues abroad and scandals at home. In Latin America alone, from 1900 to 1976, we invaded or occupied countries on an average of one every other year. John Stockwell, who sat on the National Security Council with Henry Kissinger, estimates that we have secretly overthrown twenty democracies. And while we have been mired in Watergate, Contragate, and the Savings and Loan scandal, Europe has been uniting economically and working toward political and diplomatic unity!

• When President Dwight Eisenhower left office, he warned us about the dangers of the military-industrial complex. Since that time, we have poured more money into the military-industrial complex than had previously been spent on weaponry in the entire history of the world.

• The KGB has been disgraced and communism is no longer a threat to our security as a nation. Yet we still spend an estimated $30 billion a year in our "black budget" to fund covert operations which, when uncovered, most often make us hang our heads in shame.

⊷⊰ ACTION ⊱⊶

• Support people who are communicating the spirit. Bureaucracies, governments, educational institutions and numerous officials often seem dedicated to killing the spirit. Support the efforts of small non-profit corporations and communities of faith and local educators and politicians who struggle to reform spirit-killing bureaucracies.

- Sign petitions, write letters to elected representatives and letters to editors, aware that such communication is not merely a protest, but a vital way to communicate the spirit.

- Demand an end to Cold War spending and Cold War tactics now that the Cold War is over. Support legislation to curtail the CIA's power to conduct covert operations abroad.

⊰§ SELF-INTEREST §⊱

In communicating a spirit of service to those around us, we are helping to build circles that will bring life and hope back to us.

In breathing spirit into our political and educational institutions, we are revitalizing structures that will nourish our posterity.

⊰§ MEDITATION §⊱

John Adams was not impetuous, and was slow to join the American Revolution. When he finally did sign the Declaration of Independence, he wrote to his wife Abigail, "We may rue the day, *but our posterity will not.*" John Adams had a keen sense of posterity, of how his actions would influence his children and grandchildren and future generations.

Abraham Lincoln was ambitious and wanted desperately to be president. Yet he opposed our invasion of Mexico, even though he realized it might cost him his political career. He wrote that he would do anything to get where he wanted to go — *"anything, that is, except sacrifice my principles."* His stand on the Mexican-American war forced him to drop out of politics for a time, but he returned with his principles intact.

Frances Perkins, who, as Secretary of Labor, participated in one of the greatest social reforms in American history, said that she went to Washington to serve the cause of the working people, to serve Franklin Roosevelt, but most important of all "to serve God." She was greatly sustained by the words of Christian scripture, "We know that our labor is not in vain in the Lord."

⊰⊱ CELEBRATION ⊰⊱

- Celebrate special holidays as instances of the spirit moving through history. Martin Luther King Day, Labor Day, International Women's Day, Passover, Christmas, Easter, Earth Day—all are celebrations of the victory of life over death, of freedom over slavery.

- Celebrate the victories of the environmental movement. Celebrate the victories of the poor. Celebrate whenever peace breaks out. Commemorate the surprises breaking in on history; celebrate the people who believe in a dream and a new birth of hope.

- Celebrate the birthday of Buddha who, even after enlightenment, almost despaired because he felt that no one would understand him. He finally resolved that "some will understand," and with this encouragement he went ahead and communicated his message.

- Robert Lentz is using the traditional icon form to keep the presence of Gandhi, Martin Luther King, Jr., Dorothy Day, Mother Jones, Oscar Romero and others alive among us. The icon brings the spirit of a heroine or saint present to us so that our minds and hearts can be influenced and changed. Consider gathering some pictures or mementos of your heroines and saints in a special place in your home. Or consider sending away for a catalogue of modern icons (Robert Lentz, Bridge Building Icons, 211 Park Street, Burlington, VT 05401).

✦ FOR GROUPS ✦

Have each member of the group write out a conversation with a person who has passed a spirit on to her/him (cf. page 44). Then allow time for individuals who so desire to share with the group all or part of what they have written. In conclusion, form a circle and have each person speak out loud the names of the people who have inspired him/her. After each name is called out, the group can respond, "Present in spirit."

✦ RESOURCES ✦

Hannah Arendt, *On Revolution,* Viking Press, New York, 1963. Arendt traces the history of the American, French and Russian revolutions. She observes that ever since God and divine right ceased to be the foundation legitimating governments, governments have been more easily overthrown. Hence, almost all existing governments in the world today are the result of bloody revolutions.

Penny Lernoux, *The Cry of the People,* Penguin Books, New York, 1982. Lernoux provides in-depth background on the movements of the poor in Latin America, the rebirth of Christianity and its persecution by military dictatorships, and the role of the United States government in supporting military and authoritarian regimes in Latin America.

Eugen Rosenstock-Huessy, *Out of Revolution,* Argo Books, Norwich, VT, 1969. This "autobiography" of the western world traces the revolutions that have shaped western civilization and provides amazing insights into who we are and what has shaped the world we live in.

Page Smith, *A People's History* (in eight volumes), Penguin Books, New York, 1989. This work covers the period from the American Revolution through the presidency of

Franklin Roosevelt. It reads like an engrossing novel; the text is interspersed with anecdotes and selections from letters, diaries and newspapers of the day.

John Stockwell, *The Praetorian Guard — The U.S. Role in the New World Order,* South End Press, Boston, 1991. Stockwell is the highest-ranking CIA official ever to reveal the secret workings of the intelligence agency and covert United States foreign policy. The bibliography is exceptionally valuable.

4

Becoming Part of a New Story

Hopeful Beginnings Circling the Earth

Without a vision, the people perish . . .

Those not busy being born are busy dying . . .
— Bob Dylan

Every society has within itself currents which carry it toward sterility and death. Staying spiritually alive is not a smooth process. It entails going against the current — and facing crisis, disillusionment and desperation. "To live is to change," wrote John Henry Newman, "and to be perfect is to have changed often."

Our spiritual heritage provides images of the journey we must take — from dead ends to new beginnings, from death to life, from slavery to freedom, from illusion to enlightenment. New circles of hope arise when people are "born again," when they leave slavery and addiction in search of freedom, when through suffering they learn compassion.

In our society, remaining part of the circle of greed, consumerism, and addiction leads to a dead end. Only by breaking out of the rush toward disaster and beginning to live out a radically new story do we experience fresh life and hope.

Many years ago, I began to feel depressed and dissatisfied with my own life. My feeling was akin to the times when I have turned on the television set and looked forward to watching a good program. I begin to turn the dial and look at station after station. There is no lack of choices—there are ten, maybe fifteen choices—but all seem equally empty. I even flip the dial around again thinking that I may have missed something the first time; maybe a good program was being interrupted by a commercial. But no. It is true. There are many choices, but they all seem sterile.

That was the feeling I had about my life. There were choices, but none of them seemed life-giving. There were jobs available, but they were not appealing. At the time, my wife Pat and I were able to buy a home, but nothing we looked at seemed to fit the way we wanted to live. In the supermarket, the products on display began to look the same—all equally processed with large numbers of chemical additives. The fruits and vegetables, though marvellous to look at, were sprayed with pesticides and were increasingly hybridized for shelf life and appearance, not taste. I felt depressed about life's choices—as if I were becoming part of the living dead.

Somewhere, deep within us, there was a dream of something different, but it was not clear what that "something different" was. All that was clear was dissatisfaction with the mainstream choices all around us.

We made one basic decision—not to spend our lives doing things we did not want to do just because they were the best of a bad lot. We avoided taking jobs that did not make any sense. We began following hints and suggestions—possibilities that were in no sense what we ultimately wanted, but which led us to further steps, which opened up further possibilities.

Little by little we began to put together a different way of living. We slowly left a dead story behind and became part of a story through which life and spirit could flow. We arrived at places that we would not have been able to imagine when we started out.

Frederick and Claske Franck helped with that vision. Frederick had been a doctor and a dentist who helped Albert Schweitzer in Africa. He became an artist and he and Claske built a center in upstate New York named Pacem in Terris. Their work there was an inspiration to us. I was worrying about money at the time, when I came across an interview with Pete Seeger. He said he had stopped selling his music and had begun giving it away—less money for bombs, he said. The interview stuck with me.

I had a recurrent dream of a place where new possibilities could be pursued—by ourselves and with others. That dream led us to a piece of land overlooking a little lake. We began growing much of our own food, taking better care of our health, letting the land tell us what to do next. We used recycled material for our house, built solar panels to heat the water. We had very little money, but friends helped us and we learned how to create and to live frugally.

Pat and I started a non-profit corporation called IF to help open out alternatives for ourselves and for others. We chose a modest name—IF—deliberately. We knew we could not save the world (much less understand it), but we also knew that we had possibilities to pursue that could make a contribution. Pursuing alternatives led us to a number of different activities over the years: helping seniors and the handicapped plant their own gardens, bringing people together for seminars and celebrations, using alternative sources of energy, finding work and housing and food for refugees from El Salvador, supporting women who are working with the families of the disappeared in Peru and Honduras, and working with grassroots groups and groups of women in Nicaragua, Guatemala and South Africa. We began to connect with circles of people who were giving life and hope to each other. We found that once we had pursued some possibilities, other possibilities opened out for us. Little circles of hope touched other circles and formed links with them, not according to some master plan, but simply and naturally. All we needed was the belief that if we took some steps, other steps would open out for us. H. Richard Niebuhr once said that Christianity is a vision of the world that is not true, but that may become true if it is not doubted. We have the same feeling about hope in the world: it may become real if it is not doubted, but is acted upon!

When we tried to live within the story we saw happening all around us — greed and consumerism, environmental devastation and inane entertainment — we needed to anesthetize ourselves just to get through the day. But when we began groping along trying to create a new story, we found we had something to live for. We were participating in a birth. And as we went along, we were nourished by what was being built up around us. *The path itself became life-giving.*

We have been taught that the past and the present create the future — that trends and statistical projections tell us where the world is going — but that simply is not true. The future is created by people who go against trends and projections and begin to form creative circles of life and spirit — by people who begin to live out a new story *before that story becomes history.*

Sometimes the dreams and the actions of a relatively small number of people lead to massive social movements. In the 1930s, Myles Horton had a dream of a new South, a place of brotherhood and sisterhood, a place where blacks could vote and receive a good education, where people would judge each other by their character and not by the color of their skin. He began to step out of the circle of segregation and racial discrimination and to build bridges between rich and poor, black and white.

At the time, he was considered crazy — and dangerous. But he not only pursued his vision, he began to create the new story in a small way at Highlander Folk School, the little center he had founded in Tennessee.

For decades, Highlander defied the law. It was one of the very few places in the South where blacks and whites came together for conferences, ate together and slept in the same buildings. Myles tells the story of some white farmers who came to a conference and, seeing two black men, asked Myles what the blacks were doing there. Myles replied that he didn't know, perhaps they shouldn't be there since it was a conference for farmers; perhaps they would have to leave. "Why don't you fellows go ask them what they're doing here?" They did, and they found out what Myles already knew — the black men were farmers. The white farmers were torn between their attitude toward blacks and their attitude toward farmers who were struggling like themselves. They kept quiet, and as the conference progressed, color receded into the background and they saw only fellow farmers at the meeting.

Whites and blacks at Highlander slowly began to lose their fear and mistrust of each other. In the 1930s, 40s and 50s, little circles of trust and possibility developed that later bore fruit in the civil rights movement of the 1960s.

When the civil rights movement took off, state officials descended on Highlander, took away its non-profit status and confiscated the land. Myles was deeply hurt, but he managed to smile. When they closed Highlander, he said, "They don't understand that Highlander is not just a building — it's an idea and a spirit. And you can't padlock an idea and a spirit!"

Myles talked a lot about the long haul. "If you try to create a new story in a few years, you're just wasting your time. You have to commit yourself to something for a decade at least; otherwise, you're just fooling around!"

I still remember, before 1970, taking newspapers, bottles and aluminum cans to a recycling center. The center was run by hippies and few people went there. There was abundant evidence at that time that recycling desperately needed to be done. Yet we have had to wait another two decades for recycling to become mainstream.

Americans, historian Page Smith thinks, are impatient.

They want things to happen tomorrow. Or the day after. If they devote themselves for a year or two to a cause and don't get results, they quit and say it didn't work! But change does not come so quickly. It takes thirty years for any significant social change to take place, and it takes one hundred years for such change to become an enduring part of history. It took almost thirty years to get school playgrounds established in this country—from the time a movement for playgrounds at schools began until the movement finally succeeded. And who, we might ask, could be *against* school playgrounds?

When the great new stories begin, they never seem to have much of a chance. Movements such as the struggle for the abolition of slavery, for women's suffrage and for civil rights seemed at first to arise among "fringe elements" of the society; they waxed and they waned, at times almost disappearing from sight. But time and again, they sprang up, touched the hearts of new people, and against all odds, they emerged victorious.

We recently spent a few weeks with a leader of the Sem Terra (Without Land) movement in Brazil, a country where twelve million people live in desperate poverty, without any land or means of subsistence they can call their own. Vast tracts of land in Brazil—more than enough to take care of the entire population—lie fallow. Sem Terra has a very direct approach to the problem: They occupy unused land and wait for the military to come and surround them. Then they begin to negotiate with the government. The people prepare for at least a year for these occupations. They commit themselves to refrain from violence, but they also commit themselves to courageous action. They believe that the earth is here to serve people and to be fruitful, not just to lie fallow. They believe people have a right to food and to human dignity. Four or five thousand people at a time occupy pieces of land, and once men, women and children have occupied a parcel with tents and makeshift kitchens, it is difficult for the military to disperse them or for the government to ignore them.

About twenty-five thousand families—over one hundred and twenty-five thousand people—now own their own land through the efforts of the Sem Terra movement. And once the new landowners begin to produce food, they help feed the thousands of families that are involved in subsequent occupations. Their commitment is to those who are poorer than they are.

The Sem Terra movement now touches the lives of an estimated one million people. A majority of them have been trained in non-violent action for survival—not just for their own survival, but for the survival of those who are poorer than they are. They are directly challenging a system in which up to 80 percent of the fertile land is in the hands of less than 10 percent of the population.

Movements such as Sem Terra begin with a hope and a dream, and with a few people who begin to take steps into a different future. People who follow a vision do not know if the vision will succeed. They certainly do not know *when* it might succeed. They live by faith, and they practice patience and perseverance. Dorothy Day visited Catholic conscientious objectors in American prisons during the First World War (when there were very few), during the Second World War (when there were a few more) and during the Korean War. During the Vietnam War the numbers had grown by leaps and bounds, and Dorothy was delighted to see so many young men becoming conscientious objectors. She had been at it for over fifty years, and instead of being despondent she was able to say, "We've made such wonderful progress!"

Sometimes envisioning a new story means facing terribly grim realities. In 1988, we went to visit Ninez Montenegro García, the foundress of GAM (Grupo de Apoyo Mutuo), the Mutual Support Group for the Families of the Disappeared in Guatemala. The GAM office is in a poor neighborhood in Guatemala City. Children were playing outside and we could hear their laughter. But inside the house there was tension.

In 1985, the spokesman for GAM was found dead, with his tongue cut out. A few days later, the vice-president of the organization was killed, along with her brother and two-year-old son. "GAM was less than a year old," Ninez Montenegro García told us, "when Hector and Rosario were killed. One day Rosario and I were talking to a group of visitors from Switzerland about GAM. The very next day, Rosario went for a ride with her brother and her little boy and never returned.

"Rosario's mother and I went to the Department of Investigation to make inquiries, but all they did was make fun of us. Then, later, they called us and told us we could see Rosario. When we got there, we found their dead bodies. Rosario and her brother and her little boy had all been tortured. We were terrified. After that, everyone abandoned the organization; we were the only two left. They threatened us both with death and even made threats against my five-year-old daughter. But the two of us kept going and together we enabled the organization to rise again.

"They want to eliminate GAM so that the international community can be told that all is well in Guatemala. But we have to keep the reality of the disappeared before people's eyes. We have to keep the memory alive. Every worker and every student has to be aware that behind them stand many workers and students who have struggled for justice and have disappeared." GAM now has over one thousand members who risk their lives to tell the truth about what is happening in Guatemala.

The beginning of creating a new story is admitting the grim truth of the story that we see all around us — acknowledging the sickness but refusing to remain part of the sickness. Those who deny what is happening around them through fear or inertia have no basis on which to build a future.

For many people in our society, the beginning of creating a new story means facing addiction. We grow up with the belief that if we acquire enough money or enough possessions or enough success, we will be happy. But, of course, we never can get "enough." G. K. Chesterton observed that that is why there is a lot more pleasure-seeking going on than pleasure-finding. In a society that thrives on competition and consumption, it is no wonder that alcohol and drugs are prevalent. The premise is the same: If I can get enough money and possessions, I will feel fine; or, if I can get enough alcohol or drugs, I will feel fine. Alcoholics Anonymous and Al-Anon provide healing models for our addictive society. In these groups, the terrible truth about ourselves becomes clear—we are addicted and we live in an addicted society.

Once we realize how wounded we are, we can reach out to a new source of power, which is solidarity with others and with the Whole, with that which is greater than ourselves. Life then becomes a matter of service, not a matter of stuffing ourselves with more and more things. Life can't be stuffed into us; life flows through us! We cannot find security by building more weapons; we can find security only by joining hands.

Those who struggle today to end nuclear weapons and to build peace among peoples are shaping the future direction of humanity; yet they must do so without being able to see the results of their actions. They must persevere in the midst of seeming ineffectiveness and futility. They are scattering seeds and creating swirls of life that will circulate and bear fruit in time.

Our call as part of one living, breathing humanity is to take part in the crucial struggle to create a new story in our own time. The struggle always demands faith in a dream—in a story that has not yet happened. It is in this sense that some people always have to come too early so that others can arrive on time. They have to begin to build small circles in which people can again breathe in the breath of life. They have to believe in a new story despite all that is happening around them. And they have to take the lonely steps that will help that new story become history.

We are not alone in creating a new story. Even though governments and the media largely ignore the new stories, they are being whispered, lived and expressed in songs and poems and art all over the world. The new stories give life to the world and life to the people who begin living them out.

The steps we take do not have to be enormous steps. But they have to be focused on the particular contribution that each of us can make. "Those who would do good," William Blake reminds us, "must do so in minute particulars. The general good is the plea of the scoundrel and the hypocrite." Small steps we can actually take are always better than big steps we can only think about taking.

The question for all of us is: What are the hopes and the dreams that are crucial for our own lives and our own time in history? How can we begin to take some specific steps to create a story that is different from the one we see all around us?

What Can We Do?

⚜ REFLECTION ⚜

- Jot down on a piece of paper, as they occur to you, some of the things you want to do in life. Keep the paper around, and return to it over a period of days or weeks. Don't restrict yourself. Jot down anything that comes to mind. Daydream. Don't leave things out because they seem bizarre or unrealizable.

- Are there any small steps you can take that approach some of the things you want to do? Remember, you don't have to be a success at something or make money from it in order to try it out. You don't have to become an expert. G. K. Chesterton once bemoaned the fact that "what a lot of people used to do for fun, now only a few people do for money!" Do it for fun! And remember that following our dreams nourishes us; ignoring our dreams depresses us.

❧ LEARNING ❧

In every corner of the earth, in every profession, there are people stepping out and beginning to create new stories. There are pioneers in physics, theology, farming, medicine, business, economics, energy, psychology, construction, ecology and biology. Bill Moyers's *A World of Ideas* (Doubleday, New York, 1989) describes some of them. Get in touch with pioneers and founders. Learn from them and from the direction in which they are heading. Seek out people at the edges of institutional understanding—women, Greens, people in alternative healing and alternative energy fields.

❧ ACTION ❧

• What would you like to be remembered for? What would you like to pass on to others? To whom? Are you doing it? Are there any small steps you can take to begin doing it?

• What part can you play in creating a new story?

• Are you in contact with any people who are trying to create a new story? How can you support them and become part of the story yourself?

❧ *SELF-INTEREST* ❧

Ira Progoff, a psychiatrist, likes to tell a story of a woman who wanted to return to college and get a degree, but told her psychiatrist it wouldn't be worth it because by the time she got the degree she'd be fifty. The psychiatrist replied, "And how old would you be if you didn't get the degree?"

✠{ MEDITATION }✠

Deep within us we all have a piece of good news — a bit of a new story that needs to be lived out and told. Joseph Campbell, in his lifelong study of myths and heroes, felt that a full life consists in following the call deep within ourselves.

"If you have the guts to follow the risk, life opens, opens, opens up all the way along the line. I'm not superstitious, but I do believe in spiritual magic, you might say. I feel that if one follows what I call one's *bliss* — the thing that really gets you deep in the gut and that you feel is your life — doors will open up. They do! They have in my life, and they have in many lives that I know of."

Campbell counsels us that if we play it safe and stifle the call inside ourselves, we can lose it. We can hear the music in the forest and then close our ears and forget it forever. But we will have missed the call to life, the great adventure of the spirit.

"When I wrote about the Call forty years ago," Campbell tells us, "I was writing out of what I had read. Now that I've lived it, I know it's correct. And that's how it turned out . . . It's valid."

Calls change throughout our lifetimes. Sometimes the call is not to do something, but to stop and enter a period of quiet or healing. Sometimes in the second half of our lives we can return to "paths not taken" in the first half.

Campbell reminds us that receiving a call and responding to it is not a side issue in life, but lies at the very heart of reality. Becoming sensitive to the vision and the call is the work of our lives, the source of our bliss, and the hope of the world.

❧ CELEBRATION ❧

Celebrate the past steps that gave you new life and freedom. Make these steps the theme of your birthday, or choose another day each year and celebrate them. Celebrate them especially when life is difficult and you feel depressed. Looking back at how we have responded creatively to past crises gives us strength in the present.

Every year, around Christmas-Hanukkah-Solstice, we invite friends to a Light and Darkness Celebration. We gather on the shortest day of the year, just as the light is waning, and meditate as the darkness falls over us. We light the Hanukkah candles, and in the semi-darkness we share what has been light and what has been darkness for us during the past year. Then we light the Yule log, sing carols, dance and have a festive dinner.

At another time, near Passover and Easter, we gather to share what has been slavery or addiction for us, and what has been freedom. The heart of these celebrations is what people are actually doing in their lives, what they are struggling with, and how they keep going. In this sharing, we encourage each other to persevere in following the call.

❧ FOR GROUPS ❧

Have the members of the group write down their dreams about the things they want to accomplish in life (cf. page 59). Then allow time for people who wish to do so to share some of what they have written. To conclude, form a circle and invite each person present to go to the middle of the circle, so that the group members can stretch out their hands over that person or place their hands on that person as a sign of blessing, empowerment and support. Let each person feel the blessing of the group in prayerful silence for a few minutes.

❧ RESOURCES ❧

Alternatives to the Peace Corps: A Directory of Third World and U. S. Volunteer Opportunities, Food First Books, San Francisco, CA, 1990.

Medea Benjamin, *Don't Be Afraid, Gringo, The Story of Elvia Alvarado,* Food First Books, San Francisco, 1987.

Elisabeth Burgos-Debray, ed., *I . . . Rigoberta Menchú,* Verso, New York, 1984.

Joseph Campbell, *An Open Life,* Larson Publications, Burdett, New York, 1988.

Joseph Campbell and Bill Moyers, *The Power of Myth,* Doubleday, New York, 1988.

Bill Cane, *Through Crisis to Freedom,* ACTA, Chicago, 1980.

Philip Foner, ed., *Mother Jones Speaks,* Monad Press, New York, 1983.

Myles Horton, *The Long Haul,* Doubleday, New York, 1990.

Moving into the Light

5

Stepping Out of the Lie

Circles of Truth

The truth shall make you free . . .

— Gospel of John

In Tennessee Williams's play, *Cat on a Hot Tin Roof,* the characters live out a lie. They are constantly hiding the truth about themselves and their relationships, at times pretending that everything is all right, at other times erupting into anger, violence and drunken rampages. Toward the end, Big Daddy, who is dying of cancer, finally talks to his alcoholic son, and for the first time, they tell each other the truth. At first, the truth looms as horrible and impossible, but as they face it together, it frees them. The old man accepts his cancer and begins to talk about the "smell of mendacity" that has hovered over the family for so long.

In a world that surrounds us with illusion, deceit and addiction, beginning to admit the truth to each other is a fearsome thing. The smell of mendacity has pervaded our society for a long, long time. Watergate, the Iran-Contra scandal, the Savings and Loan scandal, the addiction to drugs and alcohol, widespread poverty and homelessness, violence, racism, reliance on military solutions to world problems—these are not isolated and exceptional incidents in an otherwise healthy society. They are all part of the web of deceit and denial that surrounds us and paralyzes us and blocks the flow of spirit and truth. Lies and addictions always go together. Only by breaking out of the invisible web of lies and forming little circles of truth can we begin to live freely and hopefully.

A friend from El Salvador once told me why he had to leave his country. "The soldiers came and dragged my neighbor out of his house and killed him. As a Christian, I could not lie," my friend told me. "When people asked me what had happened, I had to say that the soldiers came and killed him. I could not say that I didn't see anything happen. I had to tell the truth—and that is why I had to leave my country." Because my friend had told the truth, the soldiers came back to his house and burned it down, leaving his niece hanging from the rafters inside. When he arrived in this country, my friend, who had been a member of one of the Christian base communities in El Salvador, kept repeating "No es justo, es pecado." It is not just; it is a sin.

In the early 1980s, Ray Bonner, a *New York Times* correspondent, began to write about what was happening in El Salvador and how the U. S. government was supporting a death-squad military that massacred its own people. Bonner was relieved of his duties as foreign correspondent for the *Times,* but he documented his charges in a book entitled *Weakness and Deceit* (Times Books, New York, 1984).

The murders of Archbishop Romero and four American church women shocked many North Americans, but the U. S. government kept supporting the Salvadoran military, claiming that the alternative was communism and a Soviet beachhead in Central America. When hundreds of thousands of Salvadoran refugees fled into Mexico and the United States, the Reagan Administration declared that the refugees were simply fleeing poverty, not oppression, and tried to round them up and send them back to El Salvador. The churches and synagogues that tried to protect the refugees were infiltrated by FBI agents. Nuns, ministers and church workers were arrested and prosecuted by government agents.

Only in 1990 did the churches finally win a lawsuit, in which the United States government was ordered to retry 150,000 Salvadoran and Guatemalan refugees because they had never received fair trials. The judge also told the Immigration and Naturalization Service that the U.S. State Department should no longer have a determining say in who is and who is not a bona fide refugee.

During the early 1980s, I gave talks with Salvadoran refugees to a number of churches and civic groups. Some people were sympathetic, but the vast majority of churches were afraid to listen to the refugees, because they feared the Reagan Administration, which had determined to silence the refugees and to punish the people who were helping them. It was for me a revelation of how fear keeps the truth from being acknowledged.

Vaclav Havel, who was imprisoned by the Communist regime in Czechoslovakia, has a very strong phrase for what he believes people must do when they face power structures that lie. People, in their daily lives and actions, must begin to step "out of the lie into the truth."

In *Living in Truth,* Havel pinpointed the basic problem in Czechoslovakia in the 1970s: that the majority of people were living within a lie — a government sponsored lie — that the society was a healthy and functioning democracy.

Nothing, he felt, could be accomplished "within the lie" — no reforms, no new political initiatives. Nothing could really be changed until people faced up to the lie and *personally* stepped out of the lie into the truth.

Most people in Czechoslovakia went along with the lie because they were afraid. They wanted to avoid trouble; they wanted to be successful. So they confined their interests to their own personal survival and their private lives. They mouthed what the government told them, and made believe the society was working even though they knew it was not.

Those who did speak out were labeled (in both east and west) as "dissidents." Havel objected to the term "dissident" because he felt it gave a false impression of what was really happening in Czechoslovakia. By drawing a line around a small group of vocal "dissidents," the government was able to isolate them from the rest of the population and treat them as misfits, as if they were the problem and were the only people who believed something was radically wrong. Whereas in reality, Havel wrote, the line needed to be drawn not around a small circle of dissidents but *through every person in Czechoslovakia.* For everyone realized that they were living within a lie; they simply found it more comfortable to remain within that lie than to speak out and suffer the consequences.

At the time Havel saw only one possible solution, one slim hope. He spoke of people in their daily actions, in their conversations, in their work, in their writing, beginning to take a step out of the lie into the truth. Such steps would not change the politics of Czechoslovakia, but they might create a climate of truth in which a new political agenda could emerge. If people continued to live within the lie, there was no hope. But if enough people stepped out of the lie into the truth, there might yet be hope (Vaclav Havel, "The Power of the Powerless," *Living in Truth,* Faber and Faber, Boston, 1989).

Twelve years after writing this essay (years during which Havel was under continual surveillance and served another prison term), the student demonstrations erupted in Prague, the military fired on the students, the people took to the streets shouting "Havel to the Castle," and Vaclav Havel became president of Czechoslovakia!

I was astounded at the parallels between Havel's analysis of Czechoslovakia and our experience of contemporary America. Although our society is more prosperous and works more efficiently, we too live within an enormous lie. The lie has many facets. One facet is that we still need a massive defense budget. The Soviet Union was the only reason given for our massive military buildup, which brought the defense budget from a level of $80 billion during the Vietnam War to a level of $300 billion during the Reagan years. But the demise of the Soviet threat seems to have made little difference. Most of the cuts announced in 1992 were cuts in obsolete or useless weapons. The Bush administration made only the cuts that were already inevitable or that it was forced to make. Meanwhile, we continue nuclear testing and we keep on producing new and more destructive weapons. The "defense" lie is subscribed to by a majority of the members of Congress. They talk about trimming the military budget, but in no way radically reducing it.

Another lie we live by is that with about 5 percent of the world's population, we can keep consuming close to 40 percent of the world's resources. George Kennan, the architect of the U. S. policy of containment after World War II, noted in a 1948 State Department document labelled Top Secret: "We have about 50 percent of the world's wealth, but only 6.3 percent of its population. . . . Our real task in the coming period is to devise a pattern of relationships which will permit us to retain this position of disparity without positive detriment to our national security." Although Kennan himself has renounced the violent means our government subsequently employed, U. S. foreign policy ever since has attempted to keep the disparity going. Our excessive consumption and domination of the poor in Latin America has brought death to other people and death to the environment.

Another lie is that we are electing our national leaders democratically. In a country where one needs four million dollars to win election to the Senate and between four hundred thousand and one million dollars to get a seat in the House of Representatives, the people are not in control of the electoral process — the corporate funders are.

Another lie is that the United States government is promoting development, democracy and human rights in Latin America and in the third world. In 1953, the CIA helped overthrow the democratically elected Mussadegh government in Iran in order to protect British and American oil interests. In 1954, the CIA overthrew the democratically elected Arbenz government in Guatemala to protect the interests of the United Fruit Company. In 1973, the CIA helped overthrow the democratically elected Allende government in Chile. In all three cases, bloody dictatorships replaced democratically elected governments. The Contra War in Nicaragua, condemned by the United Nations and the World Court at the Hague, and the propping up of the death-squad-riddled military of El Salvador have been our most recent adventures in Central America. This is what we know about. What we do not know about may be even more frightening.

John Stockwell, who ran the CIA secret war in Angola and who sat on the National Security Council with Henry Kissinger, tells us that the CIA has been involved in over three thousand major secret operations since its inception in 1947. He estimates that it has helped overthrow twenty democratically elected governments. And not only has it consistently lied both to Congress and the American people, it has devoted a large part of its resources to propaganda work intended to influence the minds and hearts of U. S. citizens. When John Stockwell was in charge of the operation in Angola, a large percentage of his CIA staff was working in the United States, influencing public opinion regarding Angola. Stockwell testifies that in reports to Congress, his boss continually lied about what was happening in Angola and about what the CIA was really doing there.

The reverberations of our actions as a nation are often hard to gauge because so many things have been done in secret. Only recently did it come to light that the CIA was involved in the original arrest of Nelson Mandela, and that CIA agents forged documents and planted arms caches in Indonesia to make it look as if the Communist party there was plotting to overthrow the Indonesian government. This successful frame-up ultimately led to the massacre of an estimated one million civilians, some of whose names were furnished to General Suharto by the CIA.

The powers that be tell very costly lies. There is a temptation to ignore the lies and escape into a world of our own making — into drugs or alcohol or television or even a spirituality that does not relate to what is going on around us. But all such escapes make us accomplices in the lies. By saying and doing nothing about the lies, we give tacit permission to the powers that be to keep on lying.

We are paying for the hypocrisy and deceit in the emptiness and cynicism of our youth, and in the drugs and alcohol that our society craves. At the present time we live in a society of massive denial and addiction. The concentration of wealth at the top of our society is now greater than it was in 1929 — before the Great Depression. One percent of the population controls about 40 percent of the wealth. And at the bottom, there are an estimated six million homeless people. The United States now has the highest infant mortality rate in the industrialized world.

Much of Congress is bought off by arms contractors and large corporations. The military-industrial complex was a major problem when President Eisenhower first warned us about it. Since that time, it has become a voracious monster, eating up over 50 percent of our tax dollars. The U. S. government is addicted to arms production, nuclear explosions and military solutions to its problems from Latin America to the Persian Gulf. We cannot admit these addictions, so we churn out propaganda and live in denial.

The addiction to drugs and to alcohol in our country can be understood only in the context of an addictive culture, where people's souls have become empty. We have been offered no dream of building a new world. Instead, we cling to the tired politics of keeping the power structures the way they are so that those in power will be able to hold onto what they have. We have no purpose except to try to hang onto what we have, to "make ourselves comfortable" until we die.

The alternative Havel offers—stepping out of the lie into the truth—is a call to a change of allegiance. We pledge allegiance to the Whole, rather than to the structures that are bringing death to the Whole. Such a radical change of allegiance is frightening, and it must be asked if such a radical change is possible.

Hannah Arendt provides us with an historical and symbolic precedent. For the western world, she tells us, the entrance of Jesus of Nazareth into history was the surprise par excellence. His coming overturned society in a way that could not have been dreamed of before it happened.

We live within a story of radical transformation. The original creed of the early Christians was "Christ is Lord" (*Xristos Kurios*) and it was spoken in direct contradiction to the creed of the Roman Empire, which was "Caesar is Lord" (*Kurios Kaiser*). The early Christians saw Jesus as universal Lord, Lord of heaven and earth, and they could not give their entire allegiance to any secular political leader.

The radical shift in allegiance that marked the decline of Caesar and the beginning of the Christian era is the same sort of shift that we are being asked to commit ourselves to today. At that time, people saw death and decay in the structures around them and they gave their lives for a new universal allegiance. The early Christians, like the Jews under Pharaoh, saw a choice between death and life. They chose life with all their hearts, believing that the power that was within them was much greater than that of the prevailing power structures in the world. They were a persecuted minority, but they prevailed. "Sacred Scriptures," both Hebrew and Christian, were part of the alternative press, because they did not side with king and emperor. They challenged the king and the empire *in the name of the Lord.*

The major media have almost always served king and empire. Most ancient literature is much like our modern mainstream press: It toes the line of the empire in which it was written. But the Hebrew prophets took a stand for God, and judged empire and king by a higher standard. This historical precedent moves the circulation of critical information from a purely "secular" into a "sacred" light. The prophets of Israel spoke out against king and empires "in the name of the Lord." One of the contributions we can make to survival and sanity is to follow their example — to speak and to listen, not in the name of the government, but "in the name of the Whole."

That is why people of conscience and communities of faith that speak out are so important at this time. The Quaker commitment to "speak the truth to power," the Jewish tradition of the prophets who challenged the kings, and the ancient Christian tradition of not capitulating to Caesar are critically important for our world. Non-profit groups that look at the world globally, such as Worldwatch, Greenpeace and Amnesty International, are acting in the spirit of this wholistic tradition, and thus provide a great service to all of us. Individuals and groups that are dedicated to the Whole and that are not paralyzed by fear of established power become vital pathways through which truth can flow.

Information that is not in the interest of the global giants cannot move quickly or freely through the mainstream press. Ferdinand Marcos was corrupt and tyrannical for decades, but for forty years we were told that he was a staunch ally and a great friend of democracy. We cannot make informed decisions unless we have access to the information we need; yet governments and multi-national corporations that have vested interests in preserving the status quo make it difficult for us to get vital information.

The major news services, which decide what constitutes news and distribute that news throughout the world, are all part of the first world and are all owned by giant corporations. The poor majorities of the world have very little say in what qualifies as news.

Dorothy Day was constantly receiving letters and clippings from people in different parts of the United States and in other countries to let her know what was going on, because she realized that the major news media are in the business of selling and are owned by multi-national corporations. Most of their news is fed to them by governments. They are afraid to alienate government sources, so they become loyal servants of their sources. Government officials know that propaganda does not have to convince people in order to be successful; all it has to do is confuse them. People who are confused do not act!

There are many sources of information available to us, if we take the time to locate them. While propaganda deadens us, the truth brings us to life. We still have a choice of life over death, of truth over deception, of freedom over addiction. The age-old choice articulated in the Hebrew Scriptures faces us once more: "Life and death are set before you today. Choose life, so that you and your descendants may live."

Lies and official stories keep the deadly power game going, but it is still the truth that can make us free. Don Ramón, a friend from El Salvador, once told me that the truth seems to be a very small thing; but if you wave even a small light in a dark cave, it drives all the bats crazy! The truth circles the earth. At first it is just a whisper, and many are afraid even to form the words. But as more people tell the truth, it becomes a crescendo, and it dispels the powers of deceit and darkness. There will always be those who prefer the darkness to the light, because their deeds are evil. But once the light of truth shines in the darkness, the darkness cannot put it out. Our call is to circulate light and truth. It is a call to action, because the truth is not so much what any one of us knows, but what two or more of us begin to do together.

What Can We Do?

This book is an "experiment in truth"—a call to live in truth. No one can *prove* that what we do comes back to us, nor that the earth is a living organism, nor that we can receive and pass on a spirit or create new stories by the way we live. All are simply invitations to become part of the circulation of life and truth. In experiments in truth, our experience slowly becomes our teacher and leads us on.

⋇⦃ LEARNING ⦄⋇

- We do not know how isolated we are from international thought and feeling. During Ronald Reagan's presidency, 365,000 people were kept out of the United States, mainly because their "ideas" were considered dangerous for Americans to hear. Among them were Graham Greene, the British novelist, and Farley Mowat, the environmentalist-author of *Never Cry Wolf.*

- Our covert wars have never been hidden from our enemies. The Nicaraguans knew what was going on. The Angolans knew what was going on. The Iranians knew what was going on. It was the *American people* who did not know what was going on and who were being deceived. Covert operations are being used not to hide things from our enemies but from our own people.

- I. F. Stone, whom Studs Terkel has called the greatest journalist of our epoch, used to say that bureaucracies put out so much information that they are bound to "let the truth slip out" at times!

I. F. Stone documented the deception of Lyndon Johnson and Robert McNamara within weeks after the Gulf of Tonkin Resolution, which began the Vietnam War. It would be a full four years before the *New York Times,* the *Washington Post* and CBS News would announce the very same findings as "exclusives."

Izzy never considered himself a special kind of journalist: "I never thought of myself as an investigative journalist, because from my boyhood I felt that every reporter investigates what he's writing about. If he doesn't, he's an idiot who just rewrites press releases."

Izzy had little regard for the secrecy of the intelligence bureaucracy. "You don't understand what's happening in history by looking through keyholes! There's a whole string of Americans who have access to secret information, some of which is quite wrong and quite false. And debates go on behind closed doors and policy is made. And those few members of Congress who have access to oversight committees become prisoners of the intelligence apparatus because they can't say what they've seen. And if they come out and criticize, they can't produce the proof, because the proof is classified. It's a disease."

I. F. Stone never received an official press corps pass in Washington, because he refused to accept advertising in his weekly newspaper. In 1941, he was ejected from the Washington Press Club for bringing a black judge to lunch there. He was finally readmitted in 1981, when he was 73 years of age.

Yet for over sixty years, Izzy revelled in ferreting out the truth and fighting for justice. Through it all, he kept up his optimism and sense of celebration. "I've had so much fun," he once quipped, "that I should be arrested!"

❧ ACTION ❧

- Clip out articles of significance and send them to friends. Write letters to editors. Keep the circulation of truth going!

- Subscribe to some of the periodicals that step out of the lie and are listed under "Resources" at the end of this chapter.

- Support programs such as Bill Moyers's public television specials and PBS's *Frontline* with Judy Woodruff. Support National Public Radio.

SELF-INTEREST

Telling each other the truth is the pre-condition for democracy. Without a free flow of information, democracy can't work. Thomas Jefferson, given the choice between maintaining a standing army and having a free press, chose a free press. Telling the truth is patriotic. Building more armaments and living in denial is not!

MEDITATION

To be a witness to the truth often means changing sides — from supporting the well-to-do to taking a stand with the poor. Oscar Romero had ties to the upper classes and the military in El Salvador when he became archbishop there. He was a good politician and kept dancing this way and that, avoiding any condemnation of the military who were killing civilians. But when the military killed Rutillo Grande, a priest who worked with the poor, Romero was deeply affected. Representatives of popular organizations came to the archbishop and asked him to condemn the murder of Father Grande. Suddenly, the archbishop stopped dancing back and forth. He spoke out, and one hundred thousand people thronged the cathedral to support him when he did so.

As the murders and massacres of peasants became more widespread and more atrocious, Romero established a Human Rights Commission to count and identify the bodies. Then members of his Human Rights Commission began to disappear. The archbishop realized that he, and everyone who associated with him, could be killed. He had changed sides. He was no longer serving the oligarchy and the military. He was now the servant of the people. "Our persecution is nothing more nor less," he wrote, "than sharing in the destiny of the poor."

The archbishop kept speaking out against social sin, starvation wages, and the repression of the people. He came to the United States and pleaded with members of Congress to stop sending arms to the Salvadoran military, because they were being used to slaughter the poor. He became an embarrassment to the CIA and to U. S. government policy.

Romero returned from Washington empty-handed, without finding any support. When he visited Rome, the pope informed him that he was thinking of taking his diocese away from him. He was alone, except for his people and his God.

It was in the midst of this loneliness that he raised his voice for the last time. He told ordinary soldiers that they did not have to obey orders that went against their consciences and against the law of God, that if ordered to kill their innocent peasant brothers and sisters, they did not have to shoot. And he addressed the military commanders directly: "In the name of God, I order you to stop the repression." These were to be the last words of the last sermon he ever gave. "In the name of God and in the name of this suffering people, whose cries rise up to heaven, louder each day, I beg of you, I plead with you, I order you in the name of God: Stop the repression."

Soon after he had spoken these words, Oscar Romero, "the voice of those who had no voice," was silenced by bullets. Mortally wounded, he spoke his last words to a stretcher-bearer: "I know who my assassins are. Tell them I forgive them."

In 1990, when the Salvadoran military killed six Jesuits and two women at the University of Central America in San Salvador, they stopped in the middle of their massacre to remove the glass from a framed picture of Romero. They then shot a bullet through Romero's head and replaced the glass on the frame. The picture still hangs on the wall of the room where the Jesuits' bodies were found.

Before he died, Romero made a prophetic statement. "If they kill me, I will rise again in the Salvadoran people." Despite massive U.S. military aid, El Salvador could not shove its poor over the edge of the earth. Despite massacres and death squad killings, the people kept rising up. It is largely due to their perseverance that a peace treaty was signed in El Salvador in 1992. If you mention the name of Romero among a group of Salvadoran peasants or workers, their eyes change and a light comes into them that lets you know that the archbishop is still alive in his people, and that the bullets and bombs have not been able to kill the truth that he proclaimed.

✦ CELEBRATION ✦

Films like *Romero, Cry Freedom, Gandhi,* and *A Man For All Seasons* are available at many video stores. Invite some friends to gather and watch the videos and celebrate the lives of these saints.

✦ FOR GROUPS ✦

Invite members of the group to jot down instances of deceit and denial that are wounding our environment, our health, and the lives of the poor. Then invite people to name some of these instances aloud and ask the group to respond "Forgive us!" Close with readings from the prophets of Israel and from recent periodicals or editorials which you judge to be truthful, courageous and prophetic.

✦ RESOURCES ✦

In Czechoslovakia, "dissidents" had to publish underground, using handwritten carbon copies to disseminate their writings. We have a flourishing alternative press that steps out of the lie into the truth, and we need to support it and be supported by it. Some examples are:

Amnesty International seeks the release of prisoners of conscience and political prisoners worldwide. It publishes both a magazine and an annual report. Amnesty International, 322 Eighth Avenue, New York, NY, 10001.

Integrities is a quarterly that envisions an integral world and tells the stories of people who are helping bring that world into existence. *Integrities,* 3015 Freedom Blvd., Watsonville, CA 95076.

Maryknoll News Notes. An extraordinary peace and justice publication that keeps you up to date on Africa, the Philippines, Latin America, the Far East, wherever Maryknoll missionaries are. Maryknoll Peace and Justice Office, 3700 Oakview Terrace, N.E., Washington, D. C. Bimonthly, short and crisp, one year: $10.

The Nation. Goes back as far as any of us can remember. Page Smith often quotes *The Nation* in his *Popular History of the United States. The Nation,* Box 1953, Marion, OH 43305. Weekly, one year: $36.

The New Yorker. Courageous editorials. Long, authoritative articles. Some of the best writing (and certainly some of the best cartoons) available in North America. *The New Yorker,* PO Box 52312, Boulder, CO 80321-2312. Weekly, one year: $32.

Unclassified. It reads like the notes for a Le Carre spy novel. But it's for real. A network of ex-CIA employees publish a newsletter called *Unclassified.* The insights into the intelligence bureaucracy are of the sort that only old spies can give us. *Unclassified,* bimonthly, $20 per year donation payable to Association of National Security Alumni, c/o Verne Lyon, 921 Pleasant Street, Des Moines, IA 50309.

6

Forming Circles of Power

Power springs up between people when they act together and vanishes the moment they disperse. . . What keeps people together after the fleeting moment of action has passed (what we today call "organization"), and what they keep alive by remaining together is power. And whoever, for whatever reasons, isolates himself and does not partake in such being together forfeits power and becomes impotent, no matter how great his strength and how valid his reasons.

—Hannah Arendt, The Human Condition

Never doubt that a small group of committed citizens can change the world. Indeed, it is the only thing that ever has.

—Margaret Mead

We come alive when we feel our power. I grew up feeling that power was outside of me—in someone else's hands. Many years ago, when the city Public Works Department began a project near our house, I wondered what they were going to do, but didn't even have the courage to ask them. I felt that they knew what they were doing and that I should not bother them.

Years later, when we moved to where we now live, it was a different story. The director of the Parks and Recreation Department had decided to hire a concessionaire to open the lake in our neighborhood to the public, a decision that people might not ordinarily have questioned. But there happened to be a little park nearby that the Parks Department had neglected for years. They didn't even pick up the garbage — and that rankled people. So instead of asking, "What are they going to do now?" a number of us began asking, "What do we *want* them to do around here?"

It was a different question, and it led to different consequences. We had a series of neighborhood meetings, we did research, we circulated petitions, and we let the county government know what we wanted. The county first tried to ignore our little group, but as we did more and more research and got more signatures on our petitions, we became a power to reckon with. After two years of struggle, we stopped the opening of the lake by the concessionaire and we forced the Parks Department to take care of the park nearby.

But the biggest change was in the attitude of the people in our neighborhood group. When we began, most of the people did not believe that we had power to do anything. Now we all feel that we have power to guide the development of this neighborhood.

When asked where the power is, we point up a ladder to the people at the top; we do not trace a circle and point to the people around us — and to ourselves. In public affairs, we have abandoned the idea of circles of ordinary citizens sitting down together and working out decisions about the future of our country. Instead, we equate democracy with elections, and let a very few people determine the future of our country. We have lost the sense of ordinary people determining the direction of our economy. Instead, we equate democracy with free enterprise and let a few people who have a lot of money manage the economy for us. We still talk about free speech, but our major media (and therefore our information) are managed and controlled, packaged and sold by multinational conglomerates. Government policies are determined at the top (usually in secret) and then "sold" to the people. The economy is managed from the top; and information is carefully controlled and disseminated from the top.

Structures at the top serve a privileged few, not the majority of people nor life on earth. In 1988 the governments of the world spent one trillion dollars for warfare and weapons ($200 for each man, woman and child on the planet) but failed to scrape together the $5 per child it would have cost to eradicate the simple diseases that killed 14 million children.

Oil spills, acid rain, a hole in the ozone layer, polluted seas and rivers are not "accidents"—things beyond our power to control. The increasing impoverishment of Africa and Latin America—the poor getting poorer and the rich getting richer everywhere—are not accidents either. They are the result of concerted power-structure policies of "killing" and "making a killing." "What is in it for *us*?" is the question at the top. The reason so much money goes to arms contractors and oil companies in this country and not to alternative energy projects or peace is that building a livable, sustainable world is *not* the corporate or government or military dream. Building a world of domination and profit is.

The present power structures—corporate, government and military—are presiding over the rapid destruction of life on earth and the increasing impoverishment of two-thirds of the world's people. They are serving not the Whole, but narrow and deadly interests.

Governments, banks, multi-national corporations and military establishments do not think round and whole. They think straight and partisan. They are perfectly willing to push poor people and living species off the edge of the earth. Radiation, massive destruction and deforestation are the by-products of their thirst for power and money. "Self-maximizing entities," Gregory Bateson called them, because their constant aim is to make *themselves* richer and more powerful.

In western law, corporations have the status of persons and can transact business as if they were persons. But they do not have the wisdom or sensitivity or conscience of persons; they are more like things than persons. This is because they are not made up of whole persons, but of parts of persons — the self-interest parts. The French still call corporations "anonymous societies" — groups without names or faces. By their very makeup, global giants lack human wholeness. They do not have wisdom or love or a sense of the Whole. They cannot join hands around the earth because their hands are always grasping. Yet they have the ear of governments; indeed, many of them are more powerful than governments. They are the main funders of politicians. They control the major media and the flow of information in the western world.

One of the first steps toward global consciousness is to recognize that the way our world is presently structured is leading us to death. We have highly developed self-interest structures, but we have very few structures that serve the Whole. The managers of corporations are hired to make money for their stockholders, not to look after the earth or the creatures within it. The military-industrial complex is a voracious monster that cannot let go of its power. The United Nations is a beginning, but it is still a gathering of self-interested nations.

We are a society of ladders, not circles. We have been schooled to look up with awe at presidents and generals and corporate executives, and to feel small in comparison to them. We have been brought up to believe that they know more than we do and therefore can make better decisions. A police inspector friend of mine used to give lie detector tests in San Francisco. When he was a young policeman, he was in awe of judges, politicians, and presidents of corporations. But after years of giving lie detector tests to politicians and corporate officials, his attitude changed considerably. "Now, when I meet important people," he told me, "I reach out to shake their hand, and can't help but wonder if I'm meeting some sort of crook!"

Hannah Arendt faces us with a very important truth: Governments above us don't have the basic power; we do (Hannah Arendt, *The Human Condition,* University of Chicago Press, Chicago, 1958). Governments may have *authority,* but we have *power.* Power rests with the people, unless they fail to exercise it. Governments have power insofar as the people allow them to exercise that power. Governments are constituted by the people and stay in power only because the people *allow* them to. Ultimately power rests, not with banks or corporations or governments but with the people *insofar as the people continue to come together, speak out and act.*

Very ordinary people have extraordinary power when they gather together, speak out and act. When Nelson Mandela visited the United States in 1990, he knew who were responsible for the changes that were taking place in South Africa: He publicly thanked the American dockworkers who refused to unload goods from South Africa, the students who demonstrated against investment in South Africa, and the people who pressured Congress to implement sanctions against the South African government. Mandela knew that the power to change things was not coming from the top—from university presidents, corporate executives and the State Department. These institutions would never have imposed sanctions unless students and workers and people of conscience in the United States compelled them to do so.

We have had the privilege in recent years of seeing how much power great masses of people have when they act together. In the Philippines, we watched the people force Marcos out of office. In Poland, in Czechoslovakia, in Hungary, and in the former Soviet republics, we saw people rise up and overturn governments, economic systems, military alliances and the entire climate of society. In South Africa, we have seen people begin to dismantle the system of apartheid.

In China, we saw first the students and then the population stand before tanks and armies; the government regained control, but the story is not over yet.

People's movements do not arise overnight. They begin with small circles of people who come together over a long period of time. Revolutions in society may take a generation or more to accomplish. A good friend who was a Catholic nun in El Salvador in the 1960s once described for me the beginnings of the Christian base community movement there. Poor people were gathered in huts, trying to read the Scriptures and apply them to their lives. People would stumble over the words and not understand the meaning of sentences. My friend said that if someone had told her at that time that these people would revolutionize their society thirty years later, she would have thought they were crazy! But these people have revolutionized and are revolutionizing Salvadoran society. And the army's massacres were not able to stop the movement. The peace accords signed in 1992 are a solemn testament to the perseverance of the Salvadoran people, who for ten years had to face a death-squad military that was receiving massive aid from the United States.

Courageous individuals and small groups come together for months and years and decades, slowly building the momentum that results in an outburst of indignation when the right time comes. Such revolutions do not create utopias, but they can and do overturn systems that are choking the life and the hope out of people.

As a planet, we are presently having the life and the hope choked out of us. And there is no response more powerful than people coming together in circles that speak out and act together—circles that eventually form links all over the world. Six or eight or ten people gathered in a living room or peace center or community of faith do not seem very powerful. But power originates from small groups that begin to take responsibility for the world around them.

In 1974, scientists theorized that chlorofluorocarbons

could be destroying the ozone layer that protects the earth from the sun's harmful rays. During the 1970s, a number of environmental groups demonstrated against aerosol sprays. Consumers joined in. Despite industry opposition and public relations campaigns, consumer boycotts were effective, and the Environmental Protection Agency began regulating the use of CFCs in aerosol sprays. But in the early 1980s, the Reagan administration claimed that ozone depletion was not a problem, and under Anne Gorsuch Burford, the EPA all but ceased working on the issue. Industry stopped working on CFC substitutes.

When Burford left EPA, some staffers within the organization began pressing the CFC issue again. The National Resources Defense Council sued the EPA in 1984, and in 1985 the EPA agreed to start formulating CFC regulations under the Clean Air Act. Then scientists discovered a hole in the ozone layer over Antarctica, and their worst fears were verified. By 1987, fears were so great and public pressure so intense that nations, in the Montreal Protocol, agreed to reduce their production of CFCs. Dupont Chemical, the largest producer of CFCs, finally announced that it would begin a gradual phase-out of the chemical in 1988. In 1992, NASA discovered that an ozone hole was ready to open up over the northeastern United States and parts of Canada and Europe. Only when faced with this imminent threat did the Bush administration agree to join other countries in stepping up the elimination of CFCs. There is now massive worldwide pressure to phase out CFCs, but the worst effects of ozone damage are yet to come.

Physicians are already predicting that potentially lethal melanoma skin cancers may strike as many as one in eighty persons in the United States by 2010. Cataracts will be common. The extent of the death and destruction we will be exposed to over the next few decades is as yet unknown, but chemists theorize that the ozone hole will take nearly a century to repair itself.

The CFC story illustrates how everyone has a part to play in the issues that affect our lives—citizens' groups, consumers, educators, scientists, politicians, people who remained within the EPA even when the Reagan administration was trying to dismantle it. The nations of the world acted only after intense organizational, legal and political pressure had been brought to bear. And industry, which had always claimed there were no practical alternatives to CFCs, is now finding an array of substitutes.

You do not have to gather "important" people together to begin to exercise power. In the early 1900s Mother Jones believed what at the time seemed incredible—that the poor immigrant masses who worked for the rich tycoons could have a say in their salaries, working conditions and health care. She led marches of women with broomsticks—miners' wives whose children did not have enough to eat. She led marches of children whose limbs had been torn off by the machinery in the cotton mills. She struck fear into the hearts of governors and legislators and corporate executives because she was not afraid. When asked what her education was, she answered that she had watched her husband and her children die—that was *her* education.

She lived long enough to see what she worked for become a reality. When she was in her nineties, she told a group of women suffragettes that they did not even have to have the vote in order to exercise their power. "I have raised hell all over this country," she said, "and all I am is an old lady with a hatpin!"

People who come together to work for peace and to establish justice on the earth are the basis of our hope for survival. In our time, we are being asked to make a new act of faith: not in governments or kings or popes, but in the power of a spirited people who commit themselves to serve the Whole.

No one can accomplish very much alone. Facing a problem alone often seems hopeless. But when a few people gather together, what was before impossible suddenly becomes possible — and the first steps become visible. If we want democracy, we have to sit down together and take charge of what is going on around us.

In order to exercise our power, we have to do something together, not just talk, not just criticize, *but do something.* As Myles Horton used to say:

> If you have too many meetings, you're just going to talk yourself out of *doing* anything! You can't figure out everything beforehand. You have to start somewhere and try something. If it works, you go along with it, and if it doesn't, you try something else. But you have to *do* something; if you're not *doing* anything, you really *aren't* anything. ... When we got started at Highlander, we didn't really know where we were going, but we knew there was a need and we knew we had to bring black people and white people together. So we got them talking together without really knowing what was going to happen beforehand. What we had to do became clear only as we went along.

In one sense it does not matter where we start. We start with something particular, with something that is not going to change the whole world but with something that is related to the larger problem. And we go from there.

John Stockwell, the former CIA agent, says that people are always asking him what to do. He refuses to give talks on what people should do, because he says the answer is simple. Gather together, become informed, speak out and act. And keep at it. That has always been the answer, and time and time again, the powers that be have been overwhelmed by the seemingly naive and inconsequential power of the people.

We have the opportunity to become part of a worldwide effort that is being waged on many fronts by extraordinarily hopeful people. To sit and watch is to court disaster. To begin to take action is exhilarating. To join hands with others — and know that people all over the world are doing the same — is to experience the joy of global brotherhood and sisterhood. What lies before us is very much like the excitement of founding a new nation. We are the potential founders of a new birth of freedom for our posterity and for all the creatures of the earth.

What Can We Do?

⊰ REFLECTION ⊱

The majority of the world's people have very little education; many cannot read or write and do not have the freedom to speak up for themselves. Most do not have access to lawyers, doctors, elected representatives or even a telephone. Many spend their energy surviving. Our education places us in the top 10 percent of power in the world. How we exercise that power depends on us.

- What groups are you part of that can take action and speak out on behalf of the Whole? What group can you join? What individuals can you sit down with and talk about forming a group dedicated to the good of the Whole? Two or three people is enough for a beginning.

- Jot down the names of people or groups you know who would be open to pursuing small steps toward exercising power. Jot down a few issues that are important to you and that could be a beginning for group action.

⊰ LEARNING ⊱

Bill Moyer, of the Social Movement Empowerment Project, has outlined eight stages which successful social movements go through. He feels that movements such as the civil rights movement, the Vietnam anti-war movement, and the anti-nuclear movement have been eminently successful. The problem is that such movements take a long time to have an impact and don't feel successful during their early stages! The following is excerpted from his own description of the stages movements go through:

1. Normal Times: Normal times are politically quiet times because the powerholders successfully promote their official doctrine and policies while hiding their actual operative doctrine and policies . . . The opposition feels hopeless because it seems that the situation will continue indefinitely, and they feel powerless to change it. Beneath the surface, however, the contradictions . . . hold the seeds for popular discontent that can create dramatic changes.

2. The Failure of Institutions: The problem and the policies of powerholders continue unabated, there is little dissent or publicity, the situation seems as if it might continue indefinitely . . . Yet the efforts of this stage can eventually be used to prove that the emperor has no clothes . . .

3. Ripening Conditions: The stage is set for a new social movement. There is a critical problem that seems to be worsening, proven violations by the powerholders, many victims, spreading discontent, historical conditions, available pre-existing networks, and an emerging new wave of grassroots opposition. Yet no one . . . is expecting the emergence of a new movement.

4. Social Movement Take-off: The take-off stage is an exciting time of trigger event, dramatic actions, passion, a new social movement, public spotlight, crisis, high hopes, and output of energy ... Within two years a majority public opinion is won. But take-off is the shortest stage. Many activists don't recognize this success. Instead, they believe that the movement has failed and their own efforts have been futile ...

5. Identity Crisis of Powerlessness: The crisis of identity and powerlessness is a personal crisis for activists ... They come to realize that the problem is more serious than they had thought, that the governmental institutions, powerbrokers, and democratic processes which they thought would help solve social problems were actually part of the problem, and that the problem can be solved only if such institutions are part of the solution. Rather than feeling depressed and powerless, activists now need to recognize the power and success of themselves and their movement ...

6. Majority Public Support: Over many years, perhaps decades, public opinion against the powerholders' policies swells to an overwhelming majority ... Almost every sector of society wants to end the problem and current policies ... But strangely, nothing seems to change. The problem continues. Congress seems unable to make decisive votes, and the central powerholders continue their policies, although with cosmetic changes. Moreover, the movement appears to be in a lull ... Over the years, however, the weight of the massive public opposition, along with the defection of many elites, eventually takes its toll. The political price that the powerholders have to pay to maintain their policies grows to become an untenable liability.

7. Success: The movement finally achieves one or more of its demands. It now needs to address some hard questions: What is success? What needs to be done next? The movement needs to recognize successes achieved, follow up on the demands won, raise larger issues, focus on other demands which are in various stages, and propose larger alternatives and a new paradigm.

8. Continuing the Struggle: Peoples' struggles with the powerholders to achieve a more democratic and human society continue indefinitely. While successful movements win some gains, they create new levels of citizen consciousness and empowerment, which generate new movements. The long-term impact of movement surpasses the achievement of their specific demands.

ACTION

Trace a movement you are involved in or identify with through the above stages. Do the stages give you a better perspective on how change occurs? Given the stage that you see the movement in, how can you best support it at this time?

Share the stages that movements go through with others who have become impatient or discouraged.

SELF-INTEREST

Freedom will continue to exist for us insofar as we exercise our freedom. Like many other things in life, if we do not use it, we lose it. It is in our own best interest to act and to exercise power.

MEDITATION

Gandhi said that we are privileged to take part in the work, but the fruits of the work are not ours to determine. The work itself is a privilege.

The Buddhists say that we must not be attached to the results of our actions.

Jesus taught that power is not for domination but for service.

Berdaev, the Russian theologian, always insisted that Utopia is not within our reach, that "the kingdom is not of this world" and cannot be established in this world. Still he insisted that we devote all our energies to establishing the kingdom in this world!

Hannah Arendt, the social philosopher, felt that the world is always heading for disaster. It is only surprise and the birth of the New that saves us!

St. Paul makes the astounding observation that God has chosen the foolish things of this world to confound the wise, and the people who seem to have no power at all to overturn the powers that be!

⊰⊱ CELEBRATION ⊰⊱

It was at the most difficult of times, just before his arrest and condemnation to death, that Jesus gathered his friends together for a celebration of thanksgiving—the first Christian Eucharist. It is at the most difficult times that we need to celebrate our hope, and to acknowledge that true power does not really belong to us—we simply share in a power that is much larger than we are. "We are only vessels of clay," wrote St. Paul. The power is not ours, it is the Lord's. At the heart of all religious celebration is the realization that a much greater power is at work within us and all around us.

⊰⊱ FOR GROUPS ⊰⊱

The difficulties we face in attempting to build a sane and sustainable world are overwhelming. While recognizing our own power, we need to rely on a power much greater than our own. Allow ten minutes or so for the group to reflect and write down what keeps them going (e.g., their faith and their hope, persons and events in their lives, sayings and symbols). Then allow time for the members of the group to share what keeps them going in the face of difficulty. If possible, depending on the makeup of the group, close with a Christian Eucharist, a Jewish Seder meal, or a ritual sharing of tea or a simple meal. Celebrate the faith of the group, its commitment, and its perseverance in hope. Celebrate also the power that is so much greater than ourselves, which we seek to be a part of as we continue our efforts to build a just, peaceful and sane world.

⊰ RESOURCES ⊱

The Amicus Journal, National Resources Defense Council, Summer 1991.

Myles Horton, *The Long Haul,* Doubleday, New York, 1990.

Bill Moyer, *The Movement Action Plan,* (Spring 1987), available from The Social Movement Empowerment Plan, 721 Shrader Street, San Francisco, CA 94117.

Forming Circles of Hope

7

Circles of Solidarity

No one will be free until all are free . . .

We get caught up in our own circles and our own concerns — our family, work, social group, faith community or club. Solidarity calls us to reach beyond those circles and form links with the marginal and the different, the poor and the persecuted, with those who are being shoved over the edge of the earth.

In 1983, we began meeting some people who were being shoved over the edge of the earth — refugees who had fled here from El Salvador. Many of them had horror stories to tell. Napoleon was teaching literacy classes on the radio when the soldiers came and killed his fellow teacher and blew up the radio station. Ramón was a Catholic catechist in a village where the army killed his fellow catechists and cut their bodies into pieces. Gregorio was a rancher whose home was used for meetings of the little Christian communities of the poor. The army came and burned his house down and left his niece hanging from the rafters. Carmela was fleeing from death threats when she saw endless piles of bodies heaped along the highway — people that had first been tortured and then killed by the soldiers. Maria had attended the funeral of Archbishop Romero where shots were fired and people were wounded as they tried to enter the cathedral.

The Reagan-Bush Administration, which supported the Salvadoran military, claimed that the refugees were Communists or terrorists, or that they were fleeing for economic reasons. The Immigration Service began arresting refugees and sending them back to El Salvador. When a coalition of churches and synagogues began harboring refugees to protect them from arrest and deportation, the Reagan Administration began arresting church workers.

We had gotten to know a number of Salvadoran refugees by the time the government arrested the church workers in Tucson, Arizona. When the first arrests were announced, we were with Don Ramón, the catechist who had fled El Salvador. He reacted slowly to the news, as if he had heard it many times before. Then he led a prayer for those who had been arrested, and placed them in the company of others who had spent time in prison—Jesus, St. Paul, Martin Luther King and Gandhi.

What struck me at the time was how calm I remained as I faced the possibility of getting arrested myself. The nourishment we were receiving from working with the refugees was strong enough to make getting arrested seem less terrifying. Don Ramón and I were giving a number of talks at churches and civic groups at the time, and the thought of his being arrested was always on my mind. But he said simply that he had been threatened with death in El Salvador for speaking the truth; he would continue to speak the truth here. It was not just a matter of gritting our teeth and going forward. The solidarity and commitment of the people around us gave us new life and energy.

The experience of being with people who are threatened and persecuted changes our perspective. At a meeting of the Families of the Disappeared of Latin America, a simple peasant man from Peru introduced himself and asked me how many members of my family were disappeared. I do not remember the man's name. I never saw him again. But I will always remember his question. It drew me, an outsider, into a momentary sense of how it feels to have family members disappeared. And although I have done very little to help the families of the disappeared, I know that to distance myself from their pain would be to greatly diminish my humanity.

We who are descendants of European settlers have a long history of fencing off sections of humanity and treating them as less than human. Men have kept women in a subservient role. The European powers treated the natives in their colonies as less than human. White North Americans have followed suit, dominating the Indians, the black slaves, the Chinese, the Mexicans and the Latin Americans.

To dehumanize the "other" is, of course, to dehumanize ourselves. Oppressors lose their own humanity when they dehumanize others. While demonstrating once in front of the U.S. Embassy in Nicaragua, Myles Horton recalled how he had demonstrated against the U.S. Marine invasion of Nicaragua in 1927—sixty years before. "We're not just here trying to help the Nicaraguans," he remarked. "What's at stake here is saving our own soul as a nation."

In the comparative comfort of the United States, it is easy to simply shove the poor and miserable of the world over the edge of our consciousness. If they do not appear on television, they do not exist for us. We have moral debates about abortion, but not about the millions of children worldwide who starve soon after they are born. We debate about prolonging life for people who are on life-support systems, but we exclude from our moral debates the hundreds of millions of people who will never have enough money to be brought to hospitals and plugged into life-support systems.

We live daily lives of separation based on age, race, sex and class. Solidarity invites us to reach across the boundaries that separate us. In their greater moments all the spiritual traditions stress solidarity. Love your enemies. Compassion. There but for the grace of God . . . The call to solidarity is a continuing invitation to step beyond where we have been.

Whoever would be the greatest among you must become as the servant of all.

The basis of solidarity is the conviction that we are somehow all brothers and sisters. This is the point of the Adam and Eve story and of the Last Judgment—we have been one humanity from the beginning, and we will be one humanity until the end!

You cannot prove solidarity. You can only test it out by living it. The living is the proof.

Adolfo Pérez Esquivel, winner of the Nobel Peace Prize, learned solidarity through suffering. When he was imprisoned by the military dictatorship in Argentina, he spent part of his eighteen months in solitary confinement, cramped into "the tube," where he could barely move his body. There was graffiti on the walls of the tube, and one in particular burned itself into Pérez Esquivel's mind. With his finger, in his own blood, a former inmate had written the words, "Dios no mata"—God does not kill.

Pérez Esquivel felt anger, outrage and depression, but ultimately determined that he would not kill his enemies; instead he would devote his life to bringing a new world into being. While in prison, Pérez Esquivel learned what consciousness and conscience are all about. In isolation, he learned solidarity. In a place of torture and death, he learned the sacredness of life. He traces his present commitment to non-violent change back to those words scrawled in blood on the wall of the tube.

Long after he got out of prison, a saying of Jesus kept haunting Pérez Esquivel. "Father, forgive them, for they know not what they do." The words made no sense. Pérez Esquivel's torturers had known *exactly* what they were doing. How could Jesus say, "They know not what they do"?

Pérez Esquivel pondered this saying for months. And suddenly it dawned on him. What his torturers did not know, what they were entirely ignorant of, was that humanity is one body, that we are brothers and sisters upon the earth. Pérez

Esquivel was merely a specimen to them; they had no idea that he was their brother. Pérez Esquivel concluded that the only way he could communicate this truth to his torturers was by forgiving them.

Solidarity with other human beings is based on what Pérez Esquivel believed—that we are brothers and sisters, that we are one human family, a family whose many members we have not met. It is a leap in faith, a breaking out of a cocoon. But without that leap, human beings will continue to kill each other.

Martin Buber, the Jewish philosopher and theologian, felt that the hope of the world rests not with people who are in the center of their groupings, but with people at the fringes — people at the outer rims of nations and cultures and faiths, who reach out across the walls that divide them.

The deaf have a wonderful sign for peace. With your right hand you reach over and clasp your left hand. Then your hands part, and your left hand reaches over and grasps your right hand. Then you join both hands for a moment, as if in prayer. Then both hands part and spread out, palms down, as if skimming over a body of water in waves of peace.

The circulation of life and spirit on the earth is choked off by the separation of people, one from another. Efforts to reach across any of these barriers are contributions to peace and solidarity. Peace comes from hands reaching out and joining each other across the boundaries that separate us. It is a continual process, a painful and rewarding process.

When ordinary Americans started going on peace missions to the Soviet Union in the early 1980s, the United States was in the midst of the biggest military buildup in world history. The Soviet Union was not only the enemy; it was the evil empire. But American citizens went and formed friendships with Soviets that are still bearing fruit today.

In our own lives, visits to Honduras, Nicaragua, Peru, Mexico and Guatemala have changed us. These countries were simply names on the map until we went there and met Lucía and Nohemy and Mary and Anabel and Rodolfo and Rosa and Rafael and Elda and Nelsa and Ticao and Marisa. When you know people and keep in contact with them, a country ceases to be a place on the map and becomes a place in your heart — a place where people you love live and struggle. Lucia writes to us about the children begging in the streets of Lima, Peru, and the malnutrition and starvation that have come in the wake of the austerity measures demanded by the International Monetary Fund. Nohemy tells us of the continuing threats people in Honduras receive for protesting the forced disappearance of members of their families. Rodolfo and Marisa keep us in contact with those who are trying to organize workers in Guatemala — and who are constantly threatened with death for their efforts.

The Indians of Ecuador have chosen a simple weaving with the colors of the rainbow in it as their flag, because it depicts the variety of nature and of all the different races woven together as one. There are countless opportunities to contribute to that weaving — to let life and spirit flow from one social class, one race, one religion, or one generation to another. Every time we reach over a gap that separates us, we are putting another stitch into that weaving. We are creating the world anew.

What Can We Do?

⊰ REFLECTION ⊱

Every time we move across a boundary that separates us — older people with younger people, rich with poor, black with brown — we are engaged in acts of solidarity.

Learning a foreign language or encouraging younger people to learn a foreign language can be a giant step in solidarity.

Steps in solidarity do not have to be dramatic, nor do they have to be taken with people far away. We can begin by reaching out to family members who are alienated or to people we know who need understanding and care.

Most of us are in touch with different groups of people who might benefit by coming together so that they can get to know each other. We have the power and opportunity to bring them together; we are potential bridges.

Jot down the names of people you can reach out to, or people from different little worlds that you can bring together.

❧ LEARNING ❧

There is no learning comparable to taking a trip to another country, or living in another culture for an extended period of time. Younger children can pick up a new language in a matter of months. College students can learn more in a year abroad than they could ever learn at home.

The following organizations sponsor regular trips which put you in touch with the struggles of the poor majorities in Third World countries and with environmental issues.

World College West promotes a global perspective and immerses all students in a foreign culture. 101 South San Antonio Rd., Petaluma, CA 94952, 707-765-4500

The Center for Global Education coordinates travel seminars to Central America, Mexico, the Philippines, the Middle East, and Southern Africa. The Center for Global Education, Augsburg College, 731 21st Avenue South, Minneapolis, MN 55454, (612) 330-1159.

Global Exchange sponsors trips to poor countries and to areas of popular struggle. 2141 Mission Street #202, San Francisco, CA 94110, (415) 255-7296.

Our Developing World sponsors study tours to Africa, Central America, Hawaii and the Philippines. 13004 Paseo Presada, Saratoga, CA 95070, (408) 379-4431.

Witness for Peace maintains a continuing presence in the most conflict-ridden countries of Central America. They sponsor short-term delegations to Israel and Palestine in which participants become nonviolent witnesses to the sources of conflict. 2201 P Street NW, Room 109, Washington DC, 20037, (202) 797-1160.

Earth Stewards Network organizes Citizen Diplomacy tours to the Mideast, the former Soviet republics, and Central America. Earth Stewards also has a tree-planting project for teenagers, and brings war veterans together from around the world to work for peace. PO Box 10697, Bainbridge Island, WA 98110, (206) 842-7986.

Elderhostel sponsors numerous educational and recreational trips for senior citizens and introduce them to different cultures and to situations with environmental significance. 75 Federal Street, Boston, MA 02110, (617) 426-8056.

The *Nature Conservancy* sponsors a number of environmental tours within the United States and to Latin America. 1815 North Lynn St., Arlington, VA 22209, (703) 841-5300.

The *Center for Responsible Tourism* publishes a Responsible Traveling Newsletter. It also provides reprints of its basic materials and good advice if you send a self-addressed stamped envelope. 2 Kensington Road, San Anselmo, CA 94960, (415) 258-6594.

❧ ACTION ☙

• Amnesty International provides us with a way to help prisoners of conscience all over the world. A prisoner of conscience from the Dominican Republic wrote the following: "When the first two hundred letters came, the guards gave me back my clothes. Then the next two hundred letters came, and the prison director came to see me. When the next pile of letters arrived, the director got in touch with his superior. The letters kept coming: three thousand of them. The President was informed.

The letters still kept arriving, and the President called the prison and told them to let me go."

You can sign up with Amnesty International to write letters, telegrams or faxes on behalf of political prisoners. You decide the number of letters you can write each month — from one to many. You can choose from different areas of concern. For example, Amnesty has a special Urgent Response Network for women prisoners. 322 Eighth Avenue, New York, NY 10001.

- *Alternatives to the Peace Corps* is a book that lists organizations that sponsor people to work for a short or an extended period of time in poor countries. *Alternatives to the Peace Corps: Gaining Third World Experience,* Food First, San Francisco, CA, 1990 (also available from Pueblo to People, 1-800-843-5257).

⊰⊱ SELF-INTEREST ⊰⊱

Pastor Martin Niemoller's famous quotation about the Nazis is a classic statement of what solidarity means for each one of us. "In Germany, they came first for the communists, and I did not speak up, because I was not a communist. Then they came for the Jews, and I did not speak up because I was not a Jew. Then they came for the trade unionists, and I did not speak up because I was not a trade unionist. Then they came for the Catholics, and I did not speak up because I was a Protestant. Then they came for me, and by that time, there was no one left to speak up."

⊰⊱ MEDITATION ⊰⊱

Our friend Lucia in Peru writes to us often. She works with the poor, with youth, with communal kitchens, with the families of the disappeared and with her local Catholic parish. A few years ago she wrote about solidarity:

If only people in North America were aware of how much they would be able to do if they had even a small sense of solidarity with other peoples: they don't know what a great loss their lack of awareness is for the entire human race. In their hands lies a great part of the wherewithal that could enable millions of people to live with dignity. Very often, I get discouraged because I cannot comprehend the indifference of many people when faced with the pain and suffering of their brothers and sisters. It simply doesn't fit into my head.

Poverty is a sickness which is killing thousands of people in a thousand different ways. I ask myself: What do North Americans do when their loved ones get sick? Don't they look for some way to alleviate the sickness, some way to cure it? Don't they rush to the doctor to find out what's wrong and to get some help? Would they let the sickness get worse and cause more suffering and end up killing someone they love?

Surely they wouldn't do things to make the sickness worse! No, I don't believe they would do this. I believe they would be concerned and feel in their very own bodies the pain of their brother or sister and outdo themselves so that the sick person could recover and return to live a full life. The sorrow we feel for those we love the most — Oh, how I wish we could feel it for all the beings of the earth. That is the only way we will be able to build a society of brothers and sisters and end the poverty which is killing so many people . . .

If North Americans knew what a painful and grinding task it is just to survive each day; if they could know how our people struggle with death every moment of their lives just to be able to survive — then they would not be so blind as to elect leaders who reinforce this kind of life for millions of people. I know it's very easy to close our eyes and shut our ears, to shut ourselves off in our own worlds. But how are we ever going to meet God? What are we going to be able to say to God?

Jesus himself tells us that whatever we do to the least of our brothers and sisters here, we do to him. And the least and the littlest ones — aren't they the poor of the world? The poor who suffer the consequences of the egoism and greed and indifference of the few? This must have been how they judged, condemned and killed Jesus — the same way that we in our day condemn and kill, when, because of indifference and our own complacency, we do nothing for the poor of the world. And I don't mean charity — charity is an easy way out, and it eases our consciences. I'm talking about eradicating the real causes of poverty, of building a just world, a world of brothers and sisters. I'm talking about making it possible for all to live a full and abundant life . . .

All in all, I do believe that the movement from death to life is gathering strength. You and your friends are an expression of this resurrection; our people, in their daily struggle, also live out this resurrection. Some years ago, we were not doing what we are doing now; there did not exist such a dedicated group of people to carry out this work. This, for me, is the victory of Jesus, the victory of life over death.

I send a big kiss to everyone, with the wish that the Lord of Life will guide and accompany you always.

Lucia

⊰⊱ CELEBRATION ⊰⊱

When we first attended the summer theology courses of Gustavo Gutiérrez in Lima, Peru, years ago, we were astounded to learn that almost everyone attending knew people who had been killed because they worked for the cause of the poor. When the poor are killed, their names do not appear in our newspapers. Archbishop Romero's name we know. We do not remember the names of the peasants who were killed with him. Yet hundreds of thousands of martyrs have died in solidarity with the poor, and the killings continue daily. November 1, All Saints Day, is an appropriate time to celebrate the lives of the martyred leaders of the poor and to proclaim our own solidarity with the persecuted of the earth.

✦{ FOR GROUPS }✦

Have members of the group prepare and present short descriptions of individuals and of movements that are struggling for peace and justice throughout the world. Have the group discuss how they already are, or how they can be, involved in similar or parallel movements. Lastly, have the group probe how they might make connections with groups or movements in other countries.

✦{ RESOURCES }✦

Basta is a publication of the Chicago Religious Task Force on Central America, which provides analyses of the situation in Central America, U. S. involvement, and directions that the solidarity movement might take. Chicago Religious Task Force on Central America, 59 E. Van Buren #1400, Chicago, IL 60605, (312) 663-4398.

Robert McAfee Brown, *Unexpected News — Reading the Bible Through Third World Eyes,* Westminster Press, Philadelphia, 1984.

Eduardo Galeano, *Memory of Fire Trilogy, I. Genesis, II. Faces and Masks, III. Century of the Wind,* Pantheon Books, New York, 1987.

The Institute for Peace and Justice provides materials for parents to help them raise their chidren with a sense of solidarity. 4144 Lindell Blvd. #122, St. Louis, MO 63108, (314) 533-4445.

Latinamerica Press provides a weekly update on developments in Latin American countries. It is strong on human rights issues and church involvment in the society. A vital source of information for solidarity. Apartado 5594, Lima 100, Peru.

Maryknoll News Notes is an extraordinary publication that keeps you up to date on what is happening to people in Africa, the Philippines, Latin America, the Far East, and wherever Maryknoll missionaries are. Maryknoll Peace and Justice Office, 3700 Oakview Terrace, NE, Washington, D.C.

Howard Zinn, *A People's History of the United States,* Harper and Row, New York, 1989. Looks at history through the eyes, not of the colonizers, but of the indigenous people who were invaded.

8

The Church Universal

Circles of Faith

The call to live a spirited life is not a call to self-satisfaction or self-complacency, but to self-transcendence. We are constantly being called out of our present existence, to form circles that do not yet exist.

Some years ago, I had a dream. I was standing alone in a small clearing amid trees and crags and grey boulders when I suddenly saw a large opening in the rocky hillside facing me. The wall of the opening was made of clear glass, as were the doors. Through the glass I could see a cavernous room with a number of people standing around talking excitedly to each other. Above the entrance, in red letters that could have been from San Francisco's Chinatown, hung a sign which said: "THE CHURCH OF THE TAI CHI."

A woman inside was beckoning to me through the glass doors. I did not recognize her, and looked around to see if perhaps she was waving to someone else, but no one else was there. I pointed to myself and motioned, "Me?" She nodded reassuringly, and again invited me in with a wave of her hand. I entered the group and felt immediately at home. At the time, I did not know the meaning of the words "tai chi," and I had no idea what the dream meant. I even took a course

110

in tai chi movement at a local college to see if the course would enlighten me, but it did not.

Years later, I realized that the dream had been introducing me to a different sort of "church." Tai chi literally means "universal wholeness." I was being invited to become part of a more universal and less structured church — part of a gathering of people who were serving "universal wholeness." They were not known to me and they did not hold regular weekly meetings. They were "hidden" and gathered at a depth "beneath the surface," but the entrance to their meeting place was open and they were easily recognized and joined once one had "located" oneself near them.

The original meaning of the word "church" (*ekklesia* for the Christians and *kahal* for the Jews) was neither a building for worship nor a weekly gathering. It was a coming together of people who were being called out of slavery to a new life of freedom. They were asked to believe in a dream, in a story that had not yet happened and seemed at the time to have not even the slightest chance of becoming history! They dedicated their lives to making this new story happen, and this was their faith.

The words *kahal* and *ekklesia,* synagogue and church, originally meant *people called out* — people called to leave the ordinary existence around them and enter a new life. Following Moses or Jesus was no ordinary life. It meant leaving security behind and becoming part of shaky and radical movements. But these movements promised an abundance of spirit and life in the future.

The existence people were called to enter *did not yet exist.* When the Jews defied the power of Pharoah and left their homes, they spent forty years wandering in the desert. They did not know where they were going and had only the food they could gather for the day. When the early Christians dared to call Jesus Lord (*Xristos Kurios*) in a world where only Caesar could be called Lord (*Kurios Kaesar*), they were seen as subverting the established political order. For this, many of them faced persecution and death. They remained a struggling group at the margins of society for a century or more. If we look at present-day Christianity or Judaism in our country, we can find in them very little resemblance to their radical roots. Most adherents are comfortable within the established order, within an existence that already exists.

For Eugen Rosenstock-Huessy, *entering a new existence that did not yet exist* meant turning his back on the prevailing institutions of his society. As a young soldier returning to Germany from World War I, he was offered a position in the government, a job as head of a major religious publishing house and a chair at the university. He agonized over the decision he had to make and then, unexpectedly, he turned down all three offers! It was years before Hitler would come to power, yet Rosenstock already recognized the smell of death in the society. He could not become part of government or church or academia. He had to reject their "dead works" in order to "serve the living God."

Only in retrospect did he fully realize what he had done. He later considered his refusal to enter these institutions his *metanoia,* his radical change of mind and heart. Turning his back on the major institutions of the society was for him the beginning of a new life in the spirit. "No social space or field exists outside the powers that be and the existing institutions are all that there is at the moment of one's *metanoia,* of one's giving up dead works."

"The words make no sense," he later wrote, "the atmosphere is stifled. One chokes. One has no choice but to leave. But one does not know what is going to happen, one has no blueprint for action. The 'decision' literally means . . . being cut off from one's own routines in a paid and honored position. And the trust that this sub-zero situation is bound to create new ways of life is our faith.

"I probably did not advance much in personal virtue by this about-face toward the future, away from any visible institution. I did not become a saint. All I received was life. From then on, I did not have to say anything which did not originate in my heart."

Institutions are good at preserving and passing on the steps humanity has already taken. But they cannot create new life. They cannot lead people into a different future. The Post Office preserves our right to communicate beyond national boundaries, which was originally a revolutionary step. The Post Office preserves that possibility for us, but if you try to get the Post Office to take any radical *new* steps, you will quickly find that such a massive and established bureaucracy will not easily budge.

People who move beyond the ordinary consciousness and conscience of religious institutions face very much the same problem. They can draw on the words and the symbols for support on their journeys. But they must not expect the institutions to create new life. The community that will support them can only be found along the way, as they themselves take steps into an unknown future.

The traditional spiritual symbols are valid. We must be born again if we are to enter into the kingdom. We must acknowledge our illusions and lies and addictions. We must become part of the people if we are to be saved. We must live by faith and hope and love. We must, somewhere along the way, die to the world that systematically exploits the earth and its creatures. To be saved we must leave deadening power structures and be born again into a new community of life and hope.

People who have moved out of their ordinary existence and committed themselves to critical but shaky enterprises are part of a community still in the making. That community is being formed, not around symbols or rituals, but around the life and death issues that the symbols have always pointed to. Symbols can easily be made into realities unto themselves and get enshrined and worshiped as if they were complete. That is why Joseph Campbell insists that myth and symbol are not about something that happened way back then.

Rather, they are a key to tell us what *we* can do now. We have keys to a possible future, but they are useless unless we act on them.

Rabbi Weisenbaum of Tucson, a leader in the Sanctuary movement that protected Central Americans who fled to this country, often told Jews that the most pain they feel in America today is in the dentist's office! The Exodus and the Holocaust, he claimed, are still taking place, but the Salvadorans and Guatemalans have traded places with the Jews. They are the ones standing up to Pharaoh and being persecuted and hunted down because they have taken a stand for justice.

In *Walking the Red Line* Deena Hurwitz introduces us to Israelis who are seeking justice for persecuted Palestinians (New Society Publishers, Philadelphia, PA, 1992). Rabbi Marshal Meyer marched with the women of the Plaza de Mayo in Argentina who were protesting the disappearance of their loved ones. He was threatened with death because he dared oppose the Argentine military government. From his roots, he knew that he was standing with the people against Pharaoh. He knew that the symbols exist only to lead us to the radical reality and call of our own time.

Brian Willson lost his legs trying to stop shipments of arms to Nicaragua. The women and children in India chained themselves to the trees so the loggers would not cut them down. Archbishop Romero told the Salvadoran soldiers they should not follow orders to shoot their peasant brothers and sisters. Chico Mendez was killed for trying to save part of the Amazon. Ninez Montenegro García risks her life for the families of the disappeared in Guatemala. These are people of extraordinary faith and courage who shake us out of our ordinary existence and face us with the life and death questions of our own moment in history. By entering an existence that does not yet exist, they open out for others the possibility of making changes in their own lives.

History is constantly providing us with opportunities for achieving enlightenment, for moving out of slavery into freedom, for being born again. We are constantly being called into a new existence, out of the lies and devastation and violence all around us. "With every breath of life," wrote Rosenstock-Huessy, "we either start afresh a time that we want to differ from the past, or we continue a time that we want to perpetuate one day more."

To take steps out of the ordinary mainstream existence always means challenging institutional understanding. Years ago, Myles Horton, founder of Highlander Folk School in Tennessee, was talking to Helen Lewis, who had been teaching at a community college in the South and getting her students involved in social action. The college, which wanted nothing to do with social action, dismissed her. She felt bad about herself and talked to Myles about it. "Institutions," Myles mused, "yes, you have to work with them. You have to work with them, but you have to push them. You push them, and they move a little bit. Then you push some more and they may move a little bit farther. Finally you push them until they get to the edge. Then you push once more — and *you* fall off!"

Among the community of those who have fallen off and the community of those who are still pushing lies the beginning of a different future. And to bring that future into being, we are called to leave the familiar world we have known.

That which gives life to the world is not confined to one place or to one group of people. It does not exist in one nationality or one religion or one economic system or one ideology. Rather, it is continually being called forth from people at the edges of different cultures and religions and nationalities and professions. The Judaeo-Christian symbols can interpret that reality for us and lead us along the way, but no one owns and controls that reality. The Spirit breathes where she will.

We are now at a point in history where massive crisis is breaking in upon us, where people all over the earth are being called to give birth to a different future. They are being called to a new level of consciousness and conscience. They are taking parallel steps on local levels for survival, for peace, and for a sustainable way of living. They are challenging the structures that have been doing violence to the earth and violence to the poor. Some are highly organized; others are simply clusters of individuals trying to live their lives in a responsible fashion. But the questions they are asking and the steps they are taking bring them beyond the group consciousness and conscience of their backgrounds. For the first time in history, we are getting a glimpse of how our actions reverberate around the world, how they affect Gaia, how the future of life on earth hangs in the balance. For the first time, we can see that pledging allegiance to the Whole, not just to a particular nation or corporation or religious institution, is the way of patriotism and piety.

Who, then, will lead us from death into new life if the institutions will not do it? Who will bring us out of the ordinary existence we see all around us, out of the hypocrisy and hopelessness and pollution and hatred and war and weapons and greed? Only those who are listening to the call and making the difficult journey. Those journeys will affect the institutions in time, but institutions seldom lead the way. Eventually, the institutions will benefit by the courage of the few—and will incorporate the values that they once felt so threatened by.

Page Smith, in his *Popular History of the United States,* describes the people who took part in the massive movement for the abolition of slavery in U. S. history. He describes how the movement arose and subsided, waxed and waned, and at times almost dropped out of existence. It was fueled by blacks and whites, by women and by runaway slaves, by people from the churches and synagogues, by humanists and by socialists, by artists and writers and politicians. When the gathering of believers reached its peak, and abolition finally became a reality, Page says simply that the "church of the abolition" disbanded.

The community of people who are "called out" gathers itself together again, and again, and again, and is still gathering itself together at this moment. People from every culture and race and nationality are struggling and living heroically, fighting for human rights and justice and peace. These are our brothers and sisters in faith. We do not know them, but we know that they are there. The people of spirit cannot be easily defined; there are no walls of separation, no "ins" and "outs." Whenever people put a fence around themselves and declare themselves a "spiritual people," they have fenced themselves in. They have made it harder to be called anywhere beyond their own enclosures.

The community of those who are called forth will always be acting from the future. They will see a new story and begin to live that story out now, before its time. They will be leaving the old forms behind in order to meet the living God. Jesus told his followers that it was better for them that he go away, because if he stayed, the Spirit could not come to them. The former ways of contact could not be allowed to become idols separating them from the Living God. The name that Yahweh gave himself, "I am who am," can just as correctly be translated "I will be who I will be." If you think you see the Buddha on the road, the saying goes, kill him.

We come to know God only as we enter an unknown future. To make an idol out of that which has already happened is to falsify God. "I will not call God Allah," the novelist Kazantzakis has the dervish say. "A name is a prison and God is free. God is too big to fit inside any name. I will not call God Allah, but AHHH."

The *ekklesia* is always on pilgrimage, always following a vision and a dream. The kingdom will never really come visibly; we will not arrive at a utopia we can see and touch and feel. "Everything good has to be done over and over again forever." Yet there is a community working incessantly to bring the kingdom into being. And we are called to be part of that community of people who are unknown to us but who are following the call into an existence that does not yet exist. For the kingdom is already among us, unrecognized but powerful.

What Can We Do?

◈ REFLECTION ◈

The question for those who would seek a spiritual path in our time is not as simple as asking what spiritual community they might be a part of. The questions go much deeper: Who am I and what am I called to do? Who can help me do that? For many this will mean leaving the darkness that is a part of their country and their church and their family background in order to follow the call. Their community will ordinarily not be ready-made, but will emerge as they move along, in pursuit of their call.

Though such people will be misunderstood and even persecuted by institutions, they will be the ones who will open out new paths for those very institutions.

◈ LEARNING ◈

In all of Nazi Germany, only one Lutheran bishop and one Catholic bishop condemned Hitler. The Vatican was silent. Yet in the little village of La Chandon in Nazi-occupied France, a community of Christians risked their lives to shelter Jews. By the end of the Second World War, the little village had sheltered five thousand Jews — one for every man, woman and child in the village.

We cannot rely on massive religious structures to lead the way in moral issues. Individuals and small groups must always challenge the larger communities of faith to live up to their call.

◆❧ ACTION ❧◆

Toward the end of her life, Dorothy Day was asked to give a talk to the American Catholic bishops. She urged them to go ahead and do what was worthwhile *before* they had gathered the money and institutional support to do so. Dorothy always acted on what she believed in. The money, the institutional support, the understanding often came years — or with her, decades — later. Page Smith, in his *Popular History of the United States,* declares that Dorothy Day almost single-handedly changed the attitude and direction of the Catholic church in the United States. And she was a lay person — and a woman — with no official position in the church!

The greatest service you can provide to a community of faith is to challenge it to live up to its call, not by complaining, but by acting on your belief and by speaking out!

◆❧ SELF-INTEREST ❧◆

"The Glory of God," St. Irenaeus wrote, "is a human being fully alive." Living life to the fullest is not only its own reward, but is the greatest contribution we can make to the life of the Whole.

◆❧ MEDITATION ❧◆

For the journey that is ahead of us, we need each other. We all can draw upon the wisdom and resources of traditional spiritual paths.

Buddhism is a way to approach addiction. Enlightenment does not happen in a vacuum. It always is enlightenment about what is going on around us. It sees through the hypocrisy and veneer and duplicity in ourselves and society.

Zen breaks us past our monomaniac way of looking at things, and brings flexibility of mind.

The Quakers have a tradition of working for peace, and of "speaking the truth to power."

The Jewish community has a five-thousand-year history of conscience. They have the riches of the prophets, and the awareness that no empire or nation can command our total allegiance.

The Christian base communities of Latin America and the Philippines see the struggle of Moses against Pharaoh and of Jesus against his enemies as their very own struggle. They see the victory of the Jewish people and of Jesus as signs that God is at work in history even now, helping the poor in their struggles to construct a new society.

The community that is being formed is not necessarily called to go anywhere; rather it is called to live differently: to shape a new vision by teaching, by writing, by scientific work, by bringing up children of the dream, by simple everyday choices. By standing with people whose lives are being threatened and by defending a threatened earth, we are living in faith, hope and love.

◆§ CELEBRATION §◆

The Hebrew and Christian Scriptures are revered as written in the name of the Lord. Yet they were produced by individuals and communities of faith amid anguish, suffering and awe. We can best follow the example of the Scriptures by celebrating people who *presently* are speaking out of their own anguish in the name of the Whole. We can also remind ourselves that our own words and actions on behalf of the Whole are sacred.

A friend of ours, an Anglican priest, prefaced contemporary readings he considered inspired as: "A reading from non-canonical Holy Scripture . . ."

◆§ FOR GROUPS §◆

Prepare a few readings from people who have spoken the truth to power, beginning with the prophets of Israel and ending with the present. Consider including specifically "sacred" writings as well as "secular" sources like World-watch, Greenpeace, *New Yorker* editorials, and so forth. Consider individuals like Helen Caldicott, Frances Moore Lappe, Ralph Nader, the Dalai Lama and others who keep speaking out on behalf of a more human world. Give thanks for the words and works of those who speak in the name of the Whole. Conclude with a chance for members of the group to share how they can write letters or articles, or how they can speak either in public or in conversations "in the name of the Whole."

◦⊰ RESOURCES ⊱◦

Eugen Rosenstock-Huessy, *I Am An Impure Thinker,* Argo Books, Norwich, Vermont, 1970.

Richard Shaull, *Heralds of a New Reformation: The Poor of South and North America,* Orbis Books, Maryknoll, NY, 1984.

9

A Spirited Economy

*In former times, the Holy Ghost unified the world.
The Holy Ghost was replaced in modern times by
electricity. What in the future will replace electricity
as the unifying factor? It will be economics.*
— Eugen Rosenstock-Huessy

*You must serve God or money. You cannot serve
both.*

When my wife Pat and her friend Alice go to Central
America to work with poor women's groups there, they usually carry with them pencils, cloth, medical supplies and other items that have been donated by friends. As they were leaving for one trip, the porter at the airport looked at their baggage and shook his head. "Where is all this stuff going?" he asked. "It's way overweight." When they explained what it was for, he told them he would see what he could do. He talked to a friend at the ticket counter, and managed to get the luggage through. When they offered him a tip, he refused to take anything. "No," he said. "I've been down there. I know what it's like. Give the money to the children there."

The porter had very little schooling, but he had a highly developed sense of world economics. He knew that we are all part of a family with terribly impoverished relatives.

Most of us have a hard time understanding economics. Gilbert Keith Chesterton said that both economics and politics were a mystery to him until one day when he looked into the eyes of a little girl in a London slum. And then it struck him — the political and economic measures that would be good for that little girl were probably right and the measures that would hurt her were probably wrong.

The word "economy" originally meant household management. A good "economist" kept up the household, provided for the family, and safeguarded its resources. Anyone who neglected the land and household, squandered the resources and didn't take care of the family was looked upon not just as a bad economist, but as an irresponsible human being.

Viewed from this standpoint, the world economy is a shambles. Forty thousand members of our world family die of starvation and hunger-related diseases every day. Our household and land are being trashed, our air is degenerating, our waterways being poisoned, our soil eroding; the hole in the ozone is expanding, our forests are being demolished, and the rich variety of species on earth is being decimated. Yet government economists tell us that things are all right. How can they say this?

Our official economists don't think round and whole; they think straight, narrow and corporate. They confine themselves to measuring production, consumption and profit. They don't calculate human misery and environmental degradation. There is no debit sheet that measures malnutrition or that tells us how much we have to pay back to the earth for the open wounds we make in it. As long as corporations are producing and making money, and consumers consuming, they say the economy is "good," no matter how fast resources are being used up and how many poisons are spewing into the air and water. Both communist and capitalist economics have killed the spirit — they have behaved as if our resources were never going to run out and as if our sewers could process an infinite amount of garbage.

The Alaskan oil spill was counted, not as a loss, but as an overall gain in our economy, because the money spent to clean it up enhanced our gross national product. Oil spilled into Prince William Sound generates more GNP through cleanup activities and lawsuits than it does if it is sold at the gas pump (Michael Closson, "Eco-conversion: Beyond Oil," *Earth Island Journal,* Fall 1990). Requiring double-hulled vessels to carry the oil is not "economically feasible" because it would be expensive. Raising the miles per gallon required for automobiles (which would eliminate U.S. need for foreign oil) is not "economically feasible" either, because it would inconvenience auto manufacturers. Our environment is expendable; corporate interests are not.

The war in Iraq was also a big boost to our GNP, because it used bombs and weapons that had to be replaced; it fostered munitions sales to Israel, Egypt, Saudi Arabia and Kuwait. The ecological disaster in Kuwait was good for the U.S. corporations that went in to rebuild and clean up. The big oil companies made money. The dead bodies, the oil slick, the air pollution and the destruction of the desert flora and fauna (which will take a minimum of one hundred years to restore themselves) are not counted in our GNP. Only the business transactions are.

Our present economy makes money, but it is squandering our resources and our inheritance. When the Dow becomes more important than the Tao, warns Frederick Franck, we are on the way to disaster. Our real wealth is not money. It is the well-being of our lives and of our planet, now and in the future. Our present economy is not conserving or replenishing our wealth — it is frittering it away in order to make money. Money for whom?

Theoretically, money circulates for the benefit of the people — the family members. But in our society, it circulates more and more for the benefit of the wealthy, the powerful and the mega-corporations. From 1977 to 1988, the annual incomes of the wealthiest 1 percent of the U. S. population rose from an average of $203,000 to $451,000, according to the Center on Budget and Policy Priorities. In the same period, the incomes of the poorest 20 percent of households dropped 10 percent. In the tax bill of 1986, taxes on the rich were drastically reduced. There is now a greater concentration of wealth at the top of our society than there was before the Great Depression of 1929.

One percent of U.S. corporations are now responsible for 87 percent of the sales (Mark Hertsgaard, *On Bended Knee: The Press and the Reagan Presidency*, Farrar, Strauss and Giroux, New York, 1988, p. 77). Government policy serves these mega-corporations by giving them tax breaks, cleaning up after them and at times bailing them out when they get into trouble.

When corporate interests have been threatened abroad, the CIA has secretly overthrown and de-stabilized governments. In the cases of Iran and Guatemala, democratically-elected governments were overthrown and replaced by ruthless dictatorships that served oil interests and the United Fruit Company.

The corporations pay politicians back by providing major funding and by helping with political campaigns. National political campaigns now depend on what corporations do best — advertising and selling on TV. Corporate America has discovered that it can "sell" even the most limited candidates, just as it has been able to sell the types of food that are least beneficial to our health.

We are enraged at drug dealers because they make money at the expense of the minds and hearts of our children. We have to start looking at other "dealers" in the same light. Poking a hole in the ozone layer in order to make money for the oil companies and the arms manufacturers just doesn't make *economic* sense.

We were told that "conservatives" were running our economic policy during the Reagan and Bush years. Between 1982 and 1992 the government went on a wild binge, spending three hundred thousand billions of dollars more than it took in—hardly a conservative policy. The deficit climbed from a little over one trillion to four trillion dollars. That period of wild expansion and borrowing will affect our lives for many years to come. Just keeping up the interest payments on four trillion dollars will drain most available money from education, health care, human services and needed improvements in the infrastructure of our country.

The task before us is to stop living in denial and begin building economic democracy—government of, by and for *the people,* not of, by and for weapons manufacturers and corporate interests.

We certainly do not have control of the economy, but we do have some control of how we live our own lives. One of the most powerful personal steps we can take is a step out of consumer addiction. Sales to consumers constitute two-thirds of our annual gross national product. We live in a world where going out and buying something gives us a temporary reprieve from meaninglessness—a temporary feeling of salvation. People go shopping just to get a fix. They buy things they don't need just to make themselves *feel* better, and advertising aids and abets their addiction. An economics without spirit simply says that the more things you have, the better off you are. But this is addiction and addiction is endless. The more we have, the more we want! Addictive behavior never fills the deepest needs within us. These needs can be filled only by creativity, love and service.

We visited China many years ago and marvelled at the frugality of the Chinese peasants. Green vegetables were planted on every inch of available soil. Nothing was wasted; the Chinese would flourish on what we throw away. Ever since then, when I buy something, I ask myself if a Chinese peasant would understand! They would smilingly approve of much that is beyond their own means, but they would strongly disapprove of waste and throwaways and impulse buying. I am very aware that the thirty dollars we spend on dinner for two is the entire monthly income of people we know in Latin America. And many other people live far below that level. In Peru, I remember the little street urchins with their noses pressed against the windows of the restaurants, watching us eat. Such memories give me a sense of proportion. The ads on television impart an outrageously false sense of proportion — they portray a life that only a few people can live. Getting in tune with world economics means feeling within ourselves the Whole situation, and beginning to live as a part of that Whole. Not with a sense of guilt or despair, but with an eye to the possibilities we have to help build a decent world — a world that is both frugal and elegant.

We cannot solve the problems of inequity in the world, but we can participate in small exchanges that ease the burden on the poor of the world. Whenever my wife goes to Latin America, we ask friends for donations of clothing, writing materials, medical supplies and other needed items. We bring supplies and cash to struggling organizations of the poor. And we try to link groups struggling for justice here with similar groups in poor countries. Little by little, connections are set up that keep people here in touch with people there. And information, solidarity and small amounts of aid begin to circulate.

How we live here ultimately affects people there. Their standard of living needs to be raised; ours needs to become more frugal. By buying appliances built to last and conserve energy, we can take important steps toward frugality. By avoiding throwaway items and items with costly packaging, we can cut down on garbage at its source. As more and more green consumer pressure is applied, we will have the chance to buy products with a green seal of approval, and to shop at stores that are discriminating in their purchases.

Another power we have as consumers is the boycotting of companies that are destroying the environment or violating human rights. Disinvestment in South Africa worked. INFACT's boycott of Nestle's products—their campaign to stop Nestle from pushing infant formula on mothers in the third world—was successful. Neighbor to Neighbor's boycott of Salvadoran coffee kept pressure on the Salvadoran government to negotiate a peaceful settlement to the civil war. INFACT's boycott of General Electric products—an attempt to stop GE from producing components for nuclear weapons—publicizes GE's "bringing bad things to life" and also puts pressure on GE to get out of the weapons business.

Besides exercising a small effect on the larger economy, we can also build up healthy economic circles around us. When we built our house in the early 1970s, our neighborhood was still an old farm area where people did things for one another. When we were building our house, Quin would say, "Don't buy that. I think we can fabricate something." Donald, our farmer friend, would say, "Don't buy pipe. I've got some pipe left over that we could use." I remember wondering if these guys ever went to the store! But I began to appreciate frugality and creativity, and the relationships of neighbors who relied on one another. People expressed heartfelt emotion with a box of apples or a loan of equipment or a helping hand. The spirit circulated in very tangible ways!

In doing business, we have learned to focus on the *relationships* involved, not just the money. Doing business impersonally is often necessary, but it does not build cooperation and trust. It takes time and care to form little economic circles of people who are reliable and whose hearts are in the right place. I more and more feel that *real* economic security consists in circles of trust and cooperation that are built up over the years.

When our home was badly damaged by the Loma Prieta earthquake in 1989, Ken Johnson, a carpenter friend, helped us put things back together. We do not know what we would have done without him. On one weekend, thirty people came to help us repair cracks in our sheet rock and paint the interior of the house. The earthquake taught us that our real security lies with circles of friends and relationships of trust.

For those who have money to invest, more and more opportunities are becoming available for putting money into circulation so that it does good — or at the very least so that it does not do harm! There are now a number of investment funds that avoid arms manufacturers and products that are harmful to the environment, and that invest only in companies that treat their workers fairly.

Many non-profit corporations are involved in economic alternatives. *Pueblo to People* makes third-world handicrafts and products available directly to us, so that the poor people who make them get a fair share of the profits.

Coop America has established a network of non-profits and businesses in the United States that are dedicated to a cooperative marketplace and to the environment.

Habitat for Humanity, which is based in local churches and communities of faith, builds houses for people who otherwise could never afford to own a house of their own. Families make a downpayment with hundreds of hours of their own labor; they make monthly money payments only after they move into their new home. Habitat homes cannot be sold for profit. They must be sold to other low-income families or sold back to Habitat. Once a Habitat home is paid for, all monthly payments go directly into building more houses. The original money gets used over and over again.

For every house built here in the United States, Habitat sets aside 10 percent of the money, which enables them to build a house for a poor family in the third world. So Habitat thinks round and whole, building links between people here and people in other countries.

Grameen Bank of Bangladesh makes small loans to very poor people — people who could never get a bank loan. The bank makes little *communities* responsible for paying back. If one person in a group doesn't repay his or her loan, the other members can no longer get loans. The bank's "loan representatives" visit remote villages and talk to people directly and teach songs and ceremonies and slogans that apply directly to the economic life of the very poor. Wisdom and love flow through their economic transactions.

The Mondragon cooperatives in the Basque region of Spain produce most of Spain's major appliances and a majority of its tools. These cooperative enterprises focus not only on making money, but also on relationships of mutual support and trust in the community. Their bank, which has 400,000 depositors, has never had a new business default on a loan. The bank carefully chooses from among groups who wish to borrow money to start an enterprise and then stays with the new enterprise, providing expertise and further funding, until it becomes profitable! All workers are owners. They not only share in the profits; they also risk their initial investment of about $6,000 if a project fails. Workers have a say in management insofar as they help select managers and boards of directors. But once selected, managers function hierarchically. The board can fire them, but it cannot interfere with their decisions!

Money is never the real bottom line—our common wealth and our relationships are. The health of our planet and our trust of one another are what really sustain our lives.

Money, business contacts, purchases, financial appeals, economic decisions are constantly flowing through our lives. To begin to see our own economic circle in the light of the larger Whole, and to begin to circulate reverence and wisdom and love and sustainability in our own little circles can help build the base for a different economics in the larger world.

What Can We Do?

⊰ REFLECTION ⊱

- Make a list of the ten richest people you know, in order of their assets. Then make a list of the ten happiest people you know, in order of their happiness. Now compare the two lists!

- In the ways that we eat, dress and live, we can work toward an elegant simplicity!

⊰ LEARNING ⊱

According to Worldwatch, the world has about 160 billionaires and perhaps 2 million millionaires. 100 million people are homeless, living on sidewalks, in garbage dumps and under bridges. The world's poorest 400 million people are so undernourished that they are likely to suffer stunted growth, mental retardation or death. Yet Americans spend $5 billion each year on special diets to lower their calorie consumption.

An economy that grinds the majority of the world's peoples into the dust and makes others billionaires simply kills the human spirit. Some people suffocate in their riches, while others drown in their poverty. Spirit cannot flow through people who gorge themselves with money, just as health cannot flow through people who get so fat that they cannot function.

If everyone used the same amount of energy per capita that North Americans do, we'd fry the planet. Yet we still talk about the "underdeveloped nations" as if they should follow in our footsteps.

⊰ ACTION ⊱

Keep pressure on your elected representatives to establish a comprehensive health care plan for all Americans. The U. S. government subsidizes the military machine, savings and loans industry, banks, oil companies and the nuclear industry; yet it does not provide accessible health care for its people. Canada and Australia are far ahead of us in this regard, as are most industrialized countries. Make the government put the health of our people ahead of weapons manufacture and corporate profits.

Arms production is not an effective means of supplying jobs for people. Teaching, health care and virtually all service sectors provide more jobs per tax dollar than does arms production. Press your elected representatives to begin serious conversion from a wartime to a peacetime economy. Arms money is desperately needed to help repair the infrastructure of our country and to provide jobs that people need.

Recycling provides more jobs for the money than either garbage incineration or landfills. Many cities contract with incineration facilities because it is an easy thing to do; all they have to do is sign a contract and send a check. Recycling, however, provides more jobs, is cheaper than incineration and is definitely healthier for the environment. Find out where your garbage goes and ask your local elected officials to avoid incineration and step up recycling.

Shopping for a Better World rates the charitable contributions and the social conscience of the corporations that produce what we buy. Colgate-Palmolive, Hershey, General Mills, Johnson & Johnson, and Kellog are among the major corporations that get high marks. Many others do not. The purchases we make constitute about two-thirds of our gross national product. We can vote with our purchases if we use this little guide (*Shopping for a Better World,* Council on Economic Priorities, 30 Irving Place, New York 10003).

ᐳᢩᴴ{ SELF-INTEREST }ᴴ∂ᐸ

In our culture, economic incentives are necessary. A friend told me that idealism never rid his property of aluminum cans, but once aluminum cans could be redeemed for a few pennies, people didn't leave them on his property any more! Most people install energy-saving alternatives because they have an incentive to do so. Pacific Gas and Electric Company of northern California is one of the most forward-looking energy companies in the country because they are given incentives for helping people save energy! For every increase in conservation, PG&E receives some of the savings. The plan is ingenious because everyone saves — consumers, corporations and the planet!

It is in our interest to pressure local utilities and state and federal government to give incentives for energy-saving.

ᐳᢩᴴ{ MEDITATION }ᴴ∂ᐸ

Abraham Lincoln was fond of telling the story about the farmer who wasn't greedy — he simply wanted the land adjoining his own.

Tolstoy told the parable about "all the land a man needs." A man was told that he would be given as much land as he could run around from sunrise to sunset. The man was greedy and he planned and practiced how he could get the last inches out of the circumference of his land. When the day came for him to run around the land, he pushed himself so hard that when he finally reached the finish line at sunset, he fell over and died. And he then received all the land that he really needed — a plot of earth for his burial.

ᐳᢩᴴ{ CELEBRATION }ᴴ∂ᐸ

At Thanksgiving time, at grace before meals, when rising or going to bed, we can express our gratitude for the riches that really matter to us. To go around the dinner table and complete the sentence, "I am thankful for ..." gives us a chance to express our appreciation of what really matters in life.

❖{ FOR GROUPS }❖

Have the members of the group jot down what they are most thankful for in life, including family and friends, community, and people who have helped them in life. Then have them jot down the names of people they are helping, or people they can help by using their skills, money or time. Allow time for people to share with each other what they are most thankful for in life. If the group so desires, it might well focus on a group effort to help a particular person or cause that is in need.

❖{ RESOURCES }❖

Circles of Exchange

Pueblo to People provides assistance to very low-income people in Central America and the Philippines, and makes the handicrafts of cooperatives available in the United States. 1616 Montrose Avenue, Houston, Texas 77006.

Coop America is an alternative marketplace that brings together a network of cooperative, democratically-managed businesses and individuals. It publishes a catalog of members' products and services. 2100 M Street NW, Suite 310, Washington, D.C. 20063, (800) 424-2667.

Habitat for Humanity accepts volunteers, donations and no-interest loans to help build houses. Contact your local group or Habitat for Humanity, Habitat and Church Streets, Americus, GA 31709, (912) 924-6935.

Reading

Susan Meeker-Lowry, *Economics as if the Earth Really Mattered,* New Society Publishers, Philadelphia, PA and Santa Cruz, CA, 1988.

Shopping for a Better World 1992, Council on Economic Priorities, 30 Irving Place, New York 10003.

Investments

The following are among the growing number of funds that provide considerable interest on your investment, but screen all investments so that they will be socially as well as economically responsible:

Calvert Social Investment Fund, 1700 Pennsylvania Avenue N.W., Washington, D.C. 20006, (800) 368-2748.

Parnassus Fund, 1427 Shrader Street, San Francisco, CA 94117, (415) 664-6812.

Pax World Fund, Inc., c/o Provident Financial Processing Corp., P. O. Box 8950, Wilmington, DE 19899, (800) 372-7827.

Working Assets Money Fund, 230 California Street, San Francisco, CA 94111, (800) 533-3863. Working Assets also provides a Visa Card and long-distance telephone service that donate a percentage of profits to good causes.

Life and Death Are Set before You

10

A Life-Giving Technology

Can wisdom be put in a silver rod, or love in a golden bowl?

—*William Blake*

Knowledge and technology, like bread, are meant to be shared, not hoarded.

—*Dorothy Day*

As I sit here writing, I can feel wisdom and love flowing through some of the technology that surrounds me. I can hear water circulating through the solar panels on the roof. The light above my desk is a new fluorescent bulb which, by the electricity it saves over its lifetime, will keep one-half ton of carbon dioxide out of the atmosphere. Outside on the porch is a solar light, which turns on automatically at night, and is recharged each day by the sun. Our flashlight and camera batteries are being recharged downstairs. They can be recharged up to 1,000 times before being discarded.

We have often said that our computer and our copy machine are the most spirited machines we own, because hopeful stories of what people are doing with their lives keep flowing through these machines. Popular leaders from Ecuador and Panama and Honduras and Nicaragua have sat at these machines and told their stories. Letters from Peru and Panama and Nicaragua and El Salvador and Guatemala and the Soviet Union have been duplicated on these machines and distributed to thousands of people. Habitat for Humanity makes use of our machines, as they help poor families build their own houses.

I look forward very soon to electric automobiles with batteries that can be recharged by solar photovoltaic panels. In the not too distant future, I have hopes for non-polluting engines that run on hydrogen fuel cells. In short, I dream of becoming more and more part of a technological circle that fosters life and conserves resources.

When the first atomic bomb blast rocked the New Mexico desert, J. Robert Oppenheimer quoted the Bhagavad Gita, "We have become as the creators and destroyers of worlds." We can now destroy in minutes what took millennia to bring into existence. Gregory Bateson felt that, *given our present attitudes,* such an advanced state of technology makes our chance of survival that of a snowball in hell.

Our present attitudes are frightening. If our technology is an extension of our *selves,* then in this society we have chosen to extend ourselves mainly as consumers and destroyers. The United States alone, according to Worldwatch, consumed more minerals between 1940 and 1976 than did all humanity up to 1940. And the consumption continues at accelerating rates.

Apart from self-funding programs, 50 percent of our tax dollars presently goes to the military, much of it for a technology of death. In the Persian Gulf war, we were shown a very precise technology that locked bombs and rockets onto their targets. We watched what in retrospect amounted to hundreds of hours of television commercials released by the government, advertising a technology of destruction. What we were not shown were the tens of thousands of Iraqi bodies mangled and buried alive as they writhed in the sand.

Human beings and technology now form a web that circles

the earth. We can no longer separate our lives and our actions from the technology which is a part of us. Years ago, people used to ask the question, "Can a computer think?" The answers were not very satisfactory until Gregory Bateson pointed out that it was the wrong question. A computer cannot think by itself. The computer operates as part of a circle that includes human beings. The same is true of all our technology. We are now part of a gigantic grid in which energy and machines are linked to human beings.

The military technology we North Americans are plugged into is killing our spirit. Like a medieval suit of armor, it weighs us down and crushes life underfoot. It prevents us from dancing and celebrating and hugging other peoples. We cannot turn our necks and see what is happening in the world around us, or even in our own cities. The infrastructure of our country keeps deteriorating because we are so obsessed with destroying external enemies. Wisdom and love and spirit cannot flow through our chemical arsenals or nuclear installations any more than they could flow through Hitler's gas ovens. Our militarism has gone a long way toward killing our spirit and our hope.

The shift we are being called to make is from an advanced technology of death to an advanced technology of life — a technology that will beat the swords into plowshares, serve humanity, and not poison our air, land and water as we move into the future.

One of the major problems we face is that we the people are not in charge of our mega-technology; the corporations and the military-industrial complex are. And presidents and many congresspersons have become sales representatives for arms manufacturers and oil companies. When over 80 percent of the American people said they wanted a freeze on nuclear weapons, President Reagan and the military-industrial complex responded with "Star Wars," which allowed the Pentagon to spend even more money on weapons. When, after the Cold War, a peace dividend was within reach, President Bush led us into a war in the Gulf, and the military-industrial complex eked out another public relations victory.

The big lie is that we need more and more sophisticated death machines. No major deviation from the big lie is tolerated. President Bush's plan to reduce our nuclear warheads contained no provision for us to stop developing new and more lethal weapons. The "experts" who appear on mainstream television are overwhelmingly in favor of a large "defense" budget. Those who are not have been relegated to the status of protestors and dissidents. Experts on peace and a sustainable world are simply excluded from the major media. "Doves" in Congress are now an endangered species; they call for only modest cuts in the defense budget! The Soviet threat was the only reason given for our massive arms buildup. But now that that threat has subsided, we are constantly creating new enemies, and pretending that the same level of threat is still there. Qaddafi, Noriega, Ortega, Castro, Saddam Hussein — all suddenly appear and disappear as threats to our national security and to the security of the world. But the real threats are seldom mentioned. We received no prior official warning about greed or corruption or the Savings and Loan scandal or nuclear safety or oil spills or militarism or racism or the ozone layer or the death of the forests and oceans. The executive branch of the government has been in denial for a long time and the media has been "on bended knee."

We have made progress on environmental issues. Most politicians now have to *talk* as if they were environmentalists. Yet most of the money appropriated by Congress for the environment has been devoted to cleaning up the toxic mess we have already made. Now we have to stop making the same mess. Stop nuclear weapons development and testing, make the military file environmental impact reports, stop the chemical and fossil fuel emissions that are destroying the ozone layer, phase out the types of agriculture and deforestation that are ruining our land. Start preventive health care for the environment.

Imagine our country spending even part of its defense billions to develop a technology of life instead of a technology of death, a technology of peace rather than a technology of war. Instead of watching our technology blow up cities, we could see cities lighted by solar photovoltaics and watch children rejoice over clean air and clear water.

There is nothing impossible about building a technology with heart — a technology that serves the planet and serves people, instead of one that poisons the planet and threatens to blow everyone up. The ingenuity that created "smart" bombs could certainly create non-polluting engines. Amory Lovins, of the Rocky Mountain Institute in Colorado, calculates that the United States, *with technology now available,* could reduce its energy use by 75 percent by the year 2000, with no sacrifice in our present lifestyle or standard of living. If we were as efficient as Germany and Japan are at this moment, we would reduce our energy costs by $200 billion per year. A switch to energy-saving light bulbs would reduce our use of electricity for lighting by about 75 percent. Raising the mpg requirement for automobiles to 40 miles per gallon (Honda is now producing a car that gets 80 miles per gallon on the highway) would eliminate our dependence on foreign oil altogether. We would not need nuclear power plants. Oil spills would become a thing of the past, Gaia would benefit, the ozone layer would benefit, all the creatures of the earth would benefit. And we would save enormous amounts of money, more than enough to take care of the national debt. What holds us back? A deep-seated addiction to growth and to oil profits — and politicians who represent neither the people nor the planet, but the military-industrial complex and multinational corporate interests.

Buckminster Fuller calculated that there are plenty of resources and technology presently available to feed and house all the people of the world adequately. What is lacking is the *political will* to do so. A very small percentage of the cost of the Savings and Loan bailout, for example, could have provided fresh, safe drinking water to all the children of the world. The United Nations Development Program estimates that $20 billion per year—about 2 percent of the global military budget—would allow everyone in the world to receive primary education and health care, family planning services, safe drinking water and adequate nutrition.

We have all the technology we need to hook our television sets into a central library, where we could choose educational courses, dramas, music and movies. We could have *real choices* in what we view. But such a system would not make money for advertisers, so it is not even under consideration. Instead, little children are being fed foolishness and violence. And advertising conditions people to buy things that are unhealthy and that they do not need.

There are refrigerators that use 90 percent less energy than the ones in our kitchens. If every home in America had an energy-saving refrigerator, we could eliminate the equivalent of eighteen nuclear power plants. The new EPA-approved woodburning stoves and fireplace inserts reduce chimney emissions by 75 to 90 percent. These are not dreams, they are realities right now. So are solar panels. A recent study by U.S. government scientific laboratories indicates that renewable sources could supply 50 to 70 percent of present U.S. energy use by the year 2030.

At present, electricity generated by wind costs about eight cents per kilowatt hour. Electricity from photovoltaic solar cells is expected to cost about ten cents per kilowatt hour by the year 2000. Where I live, in California, wind power is cheaper than conventional power today and solar electricity will be cheaper in the near future. But if you factor in the war in the Persian Gulf, the hole in the ozone layer (God only knows the ultimate cost of ozone depletion and global warming) and the enormous subsidies our government gives the oil companies, the solar option looks more and more attractive.

In our home we have replaced the lights we use most often with light bulbs that use 75 percent less energy. They last more than ten times as long as ordinary incandescent bulbs—

up to 10,000 hours. They also cut the lighting bill by about 75 percent. So, even though they are expensive, from $16 to $24 per bulb, they save money in the long run. In California, Pacific Gas and Electric Company is subsidizing these light bulbs, because their use will save the power company from constructing new plants.

Taking showers usually accounts for about 32 percent of a household's water usage. Water-saving showerheads are highly advanced, and every bit as enjoyable as water-wasting showerheads. They cut water usage by about 50 percent, and less water usage means less gas or electricity to heat hot water. Worldwatch calculates that nationwide installation of low flow showerheads would conserve as much energy as oil drilling in Alaska's Arctic National Wildlife Refuge is expected to produce. If we install these water savers and also regulate the number of times we flush the toilet, we will have cut our household water use by 50 percent.

We can live very elegantly indeed with one-quarter of the energy we are using now. Nothing is holding us back from household conservation. But unless we become politically active, the power systems that control the world's resources will bring us more wars, more weapons systems, more environmental destruction and more death.

What Can We Do?

⊰ REFLECTION ⊱

There are precedents for dismantling an oppressive technology. Popular pressure, liability costs, and nuclear disasters brought nuclear power plants to a halt in the United States, despite continued corporate and government efforts to keep building them. It is possible to bring nuclear arms production to a halt also, but it will depend on the unflinching will of persistent, highly motivated people. The United States cannot ask other countries to eliminate nuclear weapons while it is busy testing and producing more of its own.

It is a time for radically new technologies to be born. Taking lead out of gasoline was an effective measure, because it effectively reduced the amount of lead in the air. Catalytic converters, which are part of the "tail-pipe" approach to pollutants, only slow down the process that is poisoning us. If the government were to fund the development of a hydrogen engine for automobiles with even a fraction of the zeal with which it pursues new weaponry, we could have a non-polluting engine in the very near future.

Recycling glass saves some energy, but legislating standard sizes for bottles and jars would enable us to re-use glass containers without melting them down (a very energy-intensive process).

⊹❦ LEARNING ❧⊹

- In 1990, the nations of the world voted 75 to 2 to stop all nuclear bomb testing. The United States and Great Britain were the sole opposing votes.

- At the comprehensive nuclear test ban treaty meeting in January of 1991, the United States threatened to veto any resolution to stop nuclear bomb testing, and in March and April of 1991, it exploded bombs larger than the ones dropped over Hiroshima and Nagasaki at the Las Vegas test site facility. In September of 1991, after the Soviet Union announced it would stop all nuclear testing, the United States exploded two more nuclear bombs.

- From past overground testing, cancer is rampant in the Nevada desert. There is now concern that the radioactivity from underground testing may get into the aquifers and the water supply near Las Vegas.

⋇{ ACTION }⋇

Let Congress and the President know what you think about continued nuclear bomb testing and the continued development of more destructive nuclear weapons. Press them to give at least 2 percent of our military budget to the UN Development Program, so that all human beings will have the necessities of life.

Consider visiting the community of faith that stands in prayerful protest at the Nevada nuclear test site near Las Vegas. For information about events at the test site and at the Franciscan Nonviolence Center in Las Vegas, contact Pace e Bene, 1420 W. Bartlett Ave., Las Vegas, NV 89106, (702) 648-2798.

Make your home and workplace a "demonstration center," where people can see recycling and alternative technology in operation. Install the new fluorescent light bulbs and low-flow showerheads. Use paper that has the "recycled" logo on it for your stationery and envelopes. Shop green! The powers that be are not going to advertise alternative technology. We have to help do the advertising and public relations for a sane world.

⋇{ SELF-INTEREST }⋇

Rechargeable C, D, and AA batteries can cut down battery costs from nine cents to one-tenth of one cent per hour. They can be recharged up to 1,000 times, so they preserve precious resources and keep toxic materials out of our landfills. Rechargeable batteries and battery chargers (even solar chargers) are available from *Real Goods* or your local hardware store.

❖{ MEDITATION }❖

Martin Buber described divine sparks embedded in everything on earth — in tools, trees, animals, rocks, and water. The sparks, according to Hasidic legend, were remnants from the explosion of the original Glory at the time of creation. The work of human beings is to use all that is around them with reverence and awe and thus bring the sparks back to life. Once liberated, the sparks will come together to reconstitute the primal Glory. A friend of mine, after reading this passage from Buber, said that he has "seen sparks" ever since!

The sparks in the things are in need of liberation; they are prisoners with their heads bowed down to their knees. "With the good strength of our spirits" we are able to raise the holy sparks, to liberate them and enable them to return to the Glory. "When what we do happens to heaven, that is where the holy sparks are raised."

Our technology is capable of "happening to heaven," of rendering service to humanity and all the creatures of the earth. The great tragedy is that at present it is happening to hell. Buber goes on to ask if perchance there can be sparks in the sins? "In the actions of people also, even in the sins that they do, dwell holy sparks of the Glory of God. And what is it that the sparks await that dwell in the sins? *It is the turning.* In the hour when you turn on account of sin, you raise to the higher world the sparks that were in it" (Martin Buber, *Hasidism and Modern Man,* Harper and Row, New York, 1958).

Our hope lies in the "turning" — the beating of swords into ploughshares, the use of our technology to serve rather than destroy life.

❖{ CELEBRATION }❖

Celebrate technologies that are simple, elegant and non-polluting! Rejoice in small improvements that you work into your daily routine. Celebrate a cloth shopping bag! Make a ceremony out of installing new energy-saving light bulbs or solar hot water heating or recycling bins. Image the sparks that fly when you help restore even a bit of creation to its primal Glory!

⋅⧉ FOR GROUPS ⧉⋅

The dean of the Cathedral of St. John the Divine in New York City once dumped bags of garbage in the cathedral sanctuary to demonstrate to the congregation how the sacred earth is being desecrated. Have each member of the group bring an example of technology or a symbol that shows reverence for the earth (e.g., cloth shopping bags, fluorescent light bulbs, watersaving showerheads, rechargeable batteries, energy-saving appliances, food sources that are nutritious but do not deplete our resources unnecessarily). Have members of the group share information about new technologies and the things they are doing to reverence and enhance life on earth.

⋅⧉ RESOURCES ⧉⋅

Earth Island Journal keeps you up to date in the fast-moving field of alternative technology. *Earth Island Journal,* 300 Broadway, Suite 28, San Francisco, CA 94133.

Greenpeace is an extremely effective activist organization that promotes nuclear disarmament and environmental issues. It publishes an excellent bi-monthly magazine. Greenpeace, 1436 U Street NW, Washington, D.C. 20009.

The *Pacific Gas and Electric Company* has instituted a number of energy-saving programs in businesses and homes in northern California. For information: Pacific Gas and Electric Company, Energy-efficient Services, 123 Mission St., San Francisco, CA 94106.

Real Goods Catalogue, 966 Mazzoni Street, Ukiah, California 95482, (800) 762-7325.

Conclusion

What has been happening in our world can easily depress us. The power of darkness and death can overwhelm us. As I was finishing this book, I walked up the hill above our house and looked at two Valencia orange trees that had been shrivelled by a killing freeze last winter. For months, they had appeared dead. But during the summer new shoots sprouted and now a few blossoms are appearing. They will be fruitful once again.

The premise of this book has been that our hope for healing consists in the movement of life and spirit that is circulating in groups of human beings beneath the surface of governments, mainstream media and corporate existence.

If one little cell in the human body had consciousness of what it was doing, I am sure it would feel totally helpless. There are millions of cells, billions of cells. What good is one cell, among so many? But each cell is a tiny particle of the Whole. It cannot control the Whole, but it can communicate with other cells and send messages. And when it does, hundreds, then thousands, then millions of cells can react.

As premier physicist and creator of the hydrogen bomb, Andrei Sakharov enjoyed a privileged position in the Soviet Union. But as he came to realize that the government was engaged in projects that would destroy the world, he left his privileged position and joined a tiny group of dissidents. The little group often gathered at a narrow street corner where KGB vans carrying prisoners to mock trials had to slow down. The dissidents would beat their hands on the sides of the van as it slowed down, so that the prisoners inside would realize that there were some fellow human beings who knew and cared. When Sakharov was placed under house arrest in Gorky, he and his wife Yelena Bonner persisted in their struggle. When he was finally freed, despite his poor health, Sakharov insisted on running for public office. Two days before he died, he finished writing out, in his own hand, a democratic constitution for a new union of independent Soviet socialist republics. At the time Sakharov left his position of privilege, there seemed to be very little hope for disarmament and democracy in the Soviet Union. Yet Sakharov and the little group of dissidents had felt in their own hearts and souls what many millions later came to feel. Some people have to come too early, so that others can arrive on time.

We live by faith, not by sight. Millions of people all over the earth are crying out for peace, justice and a sane environment. Millions more are crying out in their hearts. The earth itself groans. The very stones cry out.

Perhaps only environmental or economic catastrophe will bring about change. Perhaps only when our own society "hits bottom" will government, corporations and people at large begin to admit the depth of our sickness. That day may not be very far off. But whether it comes sooner or later, it is crucial that new life be flowing beneath the surface. We are able to take part in, at least on a small scale, the culture that will replace the lethal culture of domination, competition and greed.

The capacity for healing on our planet and within ourselves is awesome. In nature, in history, and in our hearts healing is at work. We are ourselves wounded healers. We do the work of healing even as we feel the pain. We are always in need of encouragement to keep going. Victory is never assured. It takes a poet like Pablo Neruda to say: "We are going to win. You don't believe it, but we will!"

No one knows exactly when the turning points will come, when social, environmental and economic crises will reach their peak. We live in expectation and hope. We are part of a great pregnancy. Within this womb, a new world is gestating. As tiny cells, we circulate spirit and nourishment. Women who have carried children in their wombs know what it is to nourish. They know connectedness and the ability to live as one.

In the final book of the Christian scriptures, a woman about to give birth appears, face to face with a dragon that is waiting to devour her child. Miraculously, the child is born and whisked away to a place of safety. The child survives.

In our time, we give birth in the face of the dragon, yet we persist because we know a secret: Life and history are full of surprises. The dead come back to life. Out of the mud springs the lotus. The weak and the powerless overturn the powers that be.

As we move forward in faith and hope, changes take place within us. We become believers. We know more than we can say. We do not live in denial; we recognize the tragedy. Yet we live and love. That is the witness now. Poet Wendell Berry counsels us to plant sequoias and "practice resurrection."

This book, which I struggled over for many years, is now in your hands. We probably do not know each other. From where I stand, I hold in my heart some circles of hope. But the existing circles are much greater than I can ever imagine. Where you stand, you hold in your heart circles I cannot see. Where you breathe now, there is life I cannot feel. But we are not apart. We breathe as one and we move as one. We are all part of that wondrous Birth which is our Hope.

About the Author

Bill Cane directs IF, a non-profit corporation that probes creative alternatives and builds people-to-people bridges between the United States and Latin America. He is also editor of the quarterly *Integrities* and author of *Through Crisis to Freedom*.

Cover design: Brian Germain
Cover art: "Healing Gaia" by Ann Thiermann

Printed on recycled paper